What I Didn't Learn In Church

Transformative Truths Beyond the Pew

Rebecca Hitchcock

Thank you to my parents, Dave and Ruth Rogers, who shared Christ and His Word with me at a very young age. I am forever grateful that they made Christ and the sweet, sweet sound of worship music always the center of our home.

To my dear husband, Cam, and our wonderful five children, Connor, Caroline, Carter, Cameron, and Claudia. Now you don't have to hear me "teach." You can just read about some of my favorite topics. Thank you for supporting and encouraging me to "finish the book." I love you all dearly.

Thank you to Sloane, my coach and publisher, for guiding, teaching, encouraging, and supporting me through this writing process. Thank you to Brian Harvey and Marcy Pusey for editing all the run-on sentences and using your creativity to engage the reader. What gifts you have—I'm honored you've shared them with me. I believe it will bless many.

Lastly, thank you to all my dear friends and family who've challenged, encouraged, shared their stories, and prayed for me as I stepped into uncharted territory and followed the Holy Spirit's lead to write this book that has been in my heart for several years. I'm so blessed to have such warriors of faith in my life.

Introduction

For the past twenty-plus years, I have been a student of the Word and gathered with women primarily outside of a church building, usually in the neighborhood in which we lived. We gathered to study scripture, share life experiences, pray, and grow in our faith. Some were seasoned Christians, some never studied the Bible, some didn't have a Bible, and some were searching for the faith. But the main desire for all of us to gather was to nurture and develop deep, meaningful relationships with Jesus.

In the course of meeting with women over two decades and three states, I observed a repeated pattern, a rhetorical question I heard in each group: "Wait, what? Why didn't I learn that in church?"

As I look back, I believe that was the same question I was asking. That question was the impetus for starting the first neighborhood gathering in the suburbs of Chicago 25 years ago.

This book is my attempt to tell the stories of those lessons learned. Each chapter focuses on a different topic, each a part of my journey and that of my friends along the way. Each chapter ends with a "Selah"—an idea taken from the psalms where the reader is invited to pause, reflect, and make it personal. The Selahs invite you to prayerfully consider how you might engage with God from your own story around the lesson of the chapter.

Chapter 1
THE STORY BEHIND THE STORY

M any of my earliest memories were of being raised in the church with Sunday school, choir, church camp, youth group, and Sunday service. I was raised in very conservative denominations. The gospel message of salvation through Jesus Christ was the foundation of those churches and my life starting at age five. Fast forward to my college years, I decided to put church on the back burner. I was self-focused and loved what the world had to offer more than God. I ignored the longing inside of me to get back to church or get back to my relationship with God.

I had another longing as well. I wanted to pursue a career in the fashion industry. At age 22, a friend of my parents, the midwest fashion director of Harper's Bizarre Magazine, was kind enough to connect me with some people in the fashion industry in Chicago. Having grown up in a suburb of Indianapolis, I was ready to go explore what fashion industry opportunities might be available in a city that I loved. Not to mention, my college sweetheart and future husband, Cam, was living and working in downtown Chicago.

After a day of disappointing interviews in Chicago that were of no avail, I considered canceling the last interview. With some encouragement from Cam, I went to the interview and shortly thereafter began a career in the fashion office of Marshall Field's.

Some of the most exhilarating and memorable times while working at Marshall Field's were coordinating the fashion shows, appearing on TV segments to report the latest fashion trends, attending Fashion Week in New York City, and meeting the most eccentric and interesting people—many of whom were famous designers, celebs, and models.

I recall a very poignant memory: It was dark, anticipation in the air, an electric vibe. Lights were flashing amongst the crowd. What were we waiting for? What was all the excitement about? I was sitting with about 2000 people. Many were buyers, fashion editors, fashion directors, and celebrities from all around the world, all waiting to see which Designer Collection was going to be the buzz for Fashion Week in New York that season. The anticipation was contagious. Suddenly, bright lights shot up, the thump of music blared, and the first model strutted to the deep bass beat down the runway. Multitudes of fashion photographers were whistling, their camera bulbs flashing every second in hopes of getting the perfect shot of the fashion model icons of the '90s.

Out walked Cindy Crawford with that half smile and infamous brown birthmark on her face, Christy Turlington and her swinging bob, Naomi Campbell strutted with confidence and attitude, and many more came down the runway, each more beautiful and full of swag than the previous. You could feel the adrenaline and thrill in the crowd. The photographers yelled, "Cindy," "Naomi!" I studied the crowd and wondered why people were wearing sunglasses. Were they just too cool, or was it the bright lights?

I also observed how obsessed some were with the new fashion trends. Many in the audience wore a color shown by a designer the previous day. It was as if they were signifying that they got the trend and were now the first to sport it. I noticed another pattern. I sensed that many identified their worth and that of others in what they wore. While at Fashion Week, I had to meet with the VP of Vogue magazine. I remember her being quite warm and friendly, but her first question to me was, "Whose is that?" referring to my outfit.

I replied, "My roommate's." She laughed, and then I got it; she thought I was joking, and so then I thought, *Oh, I better laugh it off too because I'm not wearing anything designer-worthy*. I was embarrassed to tell her that most of the outfit was from the 80% reduced rack at the Gap, and yes, some of it was my roommate's. That question was one of the most frequently asked questions when working with people in the fashion industry. "Whose is that?" It summed one up by their appearance and what they wore.

I remember leaving that meeting with a heaviness in my heart. I didn't like the feeling of an outfit defining me or the fact that one's value or worth was predicated on one's appearance. I felt like Ann Hathaway's character, Andy Sachs, in *The Devil Wears Prada* (I don't subscribe to all her lifestyle choices in the movie). I was encountering real-life people who were like characters from that film—intense women who were ice cold and driven by the material world, feelings unexpressed unless in demands or anger, and many flamboyant men who wore their feelings on their sleeves. I often found myself riding their emotional rollercoasters with them, especially when they were in creative mode preparing for a fashion show and I was assisting them. I, like Andy Sachs, would go home from work and ask myself —*What am I doing in this career?*

I often told Cam that I was going to quit. His wise reply was, "Hang in there." So I did, and about that time Marshall Field's was bought out and I got promoted. I was stunned. I wasn't sure if I could do the job at such a young age, but I knew deep down this was orchestrated by God. As I was searching for fulfillment in my career I was also searching for peace. God was inviting me to draw closer to Him.

I found myself seeking Him for direction regarding my career. I started to attend a women's Bible study in downtown Chicago and I went back to church. I was finding more peace at work and questioning if my work was helping anyone. About that time I was back at Bryant Park in Manhattan for another Fashion Week. I remember looking around the white, tented room and asking God, "How many people here know you?" If God asked the Christians to stand up in this room, how many would stand? Then I wondered, *Why is that question coming up in my heart?* Maybe it was because God was on *my* heart and *my* mind so much at that particular time.

A NEW CAREER

About eight years into my career I had our first baby and a new career as a stay-at-home mother. I traded in my trendy smart suits for jeans, and my only accessory was a spit-up stain on my shoulder. Leaving my career, moving from the city to the burbs, and having a baby, I had a whole new "look" and it wasn't attractive or trendy—it was dismal. I was so broken and depressed. With so much change, a false security and identity wrapped up in my career, and some imbalanced hormones, I found myself lifeless, numb, sleepless, and an emotional wreck. I kept searching for the answer. Maybe if I could get more work or more sleep, I would feel again. If I wasn't feeling numb, then I felt anxious. I remember sitting on the floor of our office changing a diaper and asking myself, "Is this all there is?" It was so quiet; it was so mundane, and I felt so much guilt that I wasn't feeling joy when I stared into my sweet little boy's face. In that silence I remember thinking, *I don't feel anything*. It was a very frightening emotion to feel so empty. I mean, this was supposed to be one of the most joyous times of a woman's life. Yet, I felt nothing except guilt for not feeling happy. I was suffering from postpartum depression and in a desperate place. I needed healing, strength, and faith.

A TELEVANGELIST?!

Thankfully, I had grown some in my faith from the Bible study I attended. I also had prayer support from friends at church and a praying supportive family which gave me strength. I had good doctors and began to get back to health–just in time to find out I was pregnant with our second child. I was fearful after just experiencing a tough bout of postpartum depression but throughout the pregnancy, I meditated on God's promises and was determined to trust God in the process.

I recall Arline Foster, the Bible study teacher from Chicago, calling me one afternoon. She said, "I can't meet with you as often as I would like, so I want you to watch this TV evangelist. She wears big jewelry and sometimes uses double negatives, but she has a great gift for teaching the Bible." I wondered in my mind, *Watch a TV evangelist?* But Arline knew what she was talking about, so I gave it a try. It was exactly what I needed to hear and learn.

What I didn't learn at church, I started to learn from a Bible teacher on TV! Many of the subjects I was learning weren't taught in my traditional, conservative church. I couldn't get enough! I would videotape the show and watch it in the morning and afternoon. I couldn't wait to put the kids down for their afternoon naps so I could pop in the VHS tape and watch the teaching for that day. I took copious notes in my light-blue flowered journal and studied them each day, soaking in all these new truths from scripture–scripture that I had never learned in church. It was transforming my mind, my relationship with the Lord, and my relationship with family and friends. It was rejuvenating my faith. It was affecting all areas of my life. I wanted to scream from the mountaintops, "Listen to what I just learned! Did *you* ever learn this in church?!"

"WHY DON'T YOU JUST LEAD IT?"

So, maybe I didn't scream, but I talked and talked to my sweet friends, inquiring about the many truths I was learning. One of my friends had been exposed to a charismatic church growing up and could speak to the multitude of questions I had about some of these new truths I was intrigued by and learning. Several of my friends were in the same season of life. We were previously career women and chose to leave our careers to stay at home with our children. We met once a week at one of the women's churches for a book group/playgroup with our kids. With excitement bubbling within me about what I was learning from my daily TV evangelist sessions, I suggested we read *THE*

BOOK. I have to admit I was a little insecure about bringing up the idea of starting a Bible study, but my enthusiasm trumped my fear, and I suggested the idea to the group.

Shortly after, the Lord placed ten women on my heart to invite to our home on Monday evenings. After they all said "yes" I panicked and realized that we had no one to teach us! So I made an appointment with the pastor of our church and asked him if he or someone on the church staff could lead us in a Bible study. He kindly declined and said, "Why don't you just lead it?" He then said, "You will start with a small group and watch it grow."

I thought to myself, *How in the world is this going to work? I'm just learning myself, and I'm sure these women are expecting a Bible scholar or someone with experience.* The pastor knew that when the gospel is preached and we seek Jesus, the Holy Spirit will do the rest. And the Holy Spirit did indeed because we ALL sought Jesus—the only One, the only Way, the Foundation to all our questions and answers. We were all very naïve when it came to studying scripture, but we were willing to read, discuss, inquire, search, and learn. To be honest, we were clueless. We often simply looked up scriptures about topics dear to our hearts and discussed them. We prayed together and shared our doubts, hurts, victories, and needs. We longed for authenticity and real-life applicable teaching. Most of us didn't know that the Bible offered life-applicable truths for today. Some of the women in the group didn't know that they were divinely led to the group to know Christ.

I recall one woman, many years ago, confessed, "I just came to see what your house looked like, and now I'm studying the Bible learning truths I never heard in church, and my whole family of six is in a relationship with Jesus." That is just one of the fascinating testimonies of the Holy Spirit downloading transformative truths into the lives of these ten women. As each of us was growing, the group grew to about 200 women! We had to break off into several groups where other women took the challenge to facilitate groups, and to this day there are still women's groups meeting and studying God's Word in that western suburb of Chicago. Lives are still being transformed by God's Word.

WHY DIDN'T I LEARN THAT IN CHURCH?

That first gathering in the suburbs of Chicago is where I witnessed a frequent question being asked, not only by myself, but by most of the other women: "Why didn't I learn that in church?" (As you might imagine from the title of the book, I'm still hearing this question!)

I could have never guessed all the rich relationships and revelations that would come from our gatherings in the years ahead. Much of what lies in the chapters of this book came out of those times. I'd love to tell you that life has been one steady upward swing since then, but I think you know better! In fact, some of my darkest days would still lie in the years ahead of me. After our *fifth* child, I would struggle so deeply with postpartum depression and its physiologic effects that it nearly destroyed my life. It was after I passed through that season that a friend strongly encouraged me to write this book. And I ultimately became convinced that there would be others who would pass through dark times and God could encourage someone through these transformative truths.

Other parts of my story and those of many others are weaved through the chapters ahead. As you read through the lessons we learned, I imagine you'll see some of your own story too, and add your lessons to ours. Because of course, we're all learning together.

That is my hope for you: that you may identify any misconceptions you hold regarding some of these topics and discover the great freedom that comes with knowing God's truth. "Then you will know the truth, and the truth will set you free" (John 8:32).

Chapter 2

I DIDN'T LEARN TO LIVE FREE FROM SHAME!

> "Instead of your shame, you will receive a double portion, and instead of disgrace, you will rejoice in your inheritance. And so you will inherit a double portion in your land, and everlasting joy will be yours" (Isa. 61:7).

It's a shame that so many Christians, including myself, have lived a good portion of their Christian life never fully understanding that God took care of our shame at the Cross. When I had this revelation, and I stopped striving to get God to be pleased with me, my relationship with God grew exponentially. I experienced unexplainable joy and freedom. What do I mean by that? When Christ died on the Cross, He said, "It is finished" (John 19:30)! I believe this scripture has layers of meaning but in regards to Christ ridding us of our shame on the Cross I imagine God saying:

I'm not looking at all your failures and sin. Jesus, My Son took them. He is the only perfect One who could pay the penalty for your sin because He is perfect. How about that (with a smile on His face)? I'm looking at you as a *new creation* in Christ (2 Cor. 5:17). I accept you and I approve of you because you have chosen to give your life to My Son. I now see you in Christ and that is the ONLY reason I can be in a relationship with you. So why are you *still* focusing on your sin and striving to be "good enough"? Why are you carrying the heavy weight of shame when My Son already carried it and buried it? Why are you carrying that powerful, heavy feeling just because you just messed up again? Why are you carrying that painful regret because you shouldn't have said *that or* thinking I'm really mad at you now because *this* time you really messed up— you did the BIG SIN—and there is NO WAY I can forgive this one? Hello, sweet child! My Son forgave it all at the Cross. Period. Once and for all (Heb. 10)!

I had to ask myself the question—do I really believe God's Son, Jesus, paid for it *all*? Even my shame? Do you?

SHAME CLOUDS

The enemy loves for the believer to stay under what I call "The Shame Cloud"—to feel unworthy, heavy-laden, and guilty. The enemy loves to kill, steal, and destroy any growth or truth that the Christian believes. One of the most effective ways he does that is in our thought life, whispering lies that God is mad at us. Stealing our joy and peace when circumstances in our life might be chaotic or going wrong. Accusing God of absence in our trials. Shame clouds our perspective and clouds the truth about what God thinks about us as His beloved children.

MY STORY

I started carrying shame as young as five years old, but I wasn't sure why. It wasn't until I was in my thirties that I realized this Shame Cloud, which had hovered over me since my youth, began from an incident of sexual assault by a 16-year-old male teen. Our family was helping at a Christian home for troubled youth when I was five years old, and I was a victim of a sexual assault incident while serving there. RAINN, the nation's largest sexual assault helpline, states that every 69 seconds an American is sexually assaulted. And every 9 minutes that victim is a child.

I had buried that memory for years until I had our first child. I carried so much shame, guilt, and feelings of dirtiness from that moment and for years thereafter as a young girl. Throughout elementary school, my mind would ruminate on the incident, and that ominous dark Shame Cloud would hover over me. Sometimes the thoughts of shame would make me physically sick to my stomach, and I would constantly ask God to forgive me. Shame is a powerful emotion that can even hurt us physically. I'm certain Jesus's heart broke that His little girl, who was a victim of sexual abuse, carried not just pain, but *so much guilt*. I'm confident that there are hundreds of thousands of similar stories of children living under Shame Clouds throughout their childhood, and my prayer is that they discover that Jesus took their shame and offered freedom, peace, and joy in exchange.

EVERYONE'S GOT SOMETHING THEY'RE CARRYING

In over 20 years of gathering with hundreds of women, *shame* was one of the most commonly hidden, powerful emotions each one of us carried. It was like an accessory that we didn't even realize we were wearing. It was like our handbag designed by Shame. We felt wrong, unworthy of God's acceptance because of something we did or that had been done to us. I believe God knew His people would experience shame and oftentimes not even realize that they were holding onto such a toxic emotion. When we operate with a shame-based perspective we often find ourselves in overdrive, striving for acceptance and approval from others or from what we accomplish. Society nods acceptance and approval at us when we achieve certain benchmarks or status. We are applauded when we fulfill other people's expectations. When we don't, we are booed. It's human nature. I mean, just think of the visual signals we give to our kids or loved ones that say, "You are not approved or accepted." The eye roll. The heavy sigh. We don't even realize we are giving off visual signals of disapproval. We perpetuate the cycle of longing to be accepted and approved by others.

I believe it's on steroids today. Just look at the time spent posting the perfect picture on Instagram. The creative direction and effort spent on posting the most exotic family vacations on social media for all to see. Time is even spent taking pictures of the food we eat for dinner. I didn't even know anyone cared about how beautiful my meal was! We advertise to the world how wonderful our life is and how beautiful our families are and capture it in a photo for all to see that we are approved of and accepted. *When the truth is, in Christ, we are completely accepted by the Creator Himself.* What a beautiful picture to post! Beloved, you are accepted and approved by God because His Son took our shame on the Cross. You are shame-free.

PHARISEE = SHAME

My grandfather was a Russian Baptist pastor, and he loved the Lord and showed his grandchildren much love, but there was always an undercurrent of "only being accepted and approved" when you did what God wanted you to do. Be a "good Christian" or else. Scripture tells us that no one can be justified in God's eyes by reliance upon the law (Gal. 3:11), and to bear shame because we can't keep the law is dismal and damaging. We can never do the "good Christian" thing perfectly, and God knew it. The law was given to expose our sin and to usher in the need for a Savior who was perfect and who did the "good Christian" thing perfectly. The legalistic teaching of the Pharisees is sadly still in the church today, and I believe that could be why so many believers are stuck in shame.

Another one of satan's greatest weapons is stated in Hosea 4:6, "My people are being destroyed for their lack of knowledge." Lacking knowledge or not understanding in scripture that Christ took our shame and in exchange offered us freedom, joy, and peace is the good news satan doesn't want us to grasp. Instead, the enemy would like us to walk in condemnation and guilt. Deceiving us into thinking we need to "pay" for the sin that we committed. or better yet, punish ourselves. If you're the enemy, and you want to destroy the work of what Jesus did on the Cross, why not start with shaming people and whispering in their ears,

"You are not forgiven." "How could God ever forgive and accept you for_____?" You fill in the blank.

As I mentioned, Shame Clouds hovered over many of us in the groups of women I walked with through the years. Stories of sexual abuse, abortion, adultery, divorce, physical abuse, and food addictions were not uncommon. Self-scorn and low self-esteem were the result of our wounds. What baffled all of us was that many of us *didn't actually believe* the truth in Isaiah 61: "Instead of your shame, you will receive a double portion, And instead of disgrace, you will rejoice in your inheritance. And so you will inherit a double portion in your land, and everlasting joy will be yours" (Isa. 61:7). It was easier to believe what we felt and not rejoice in our inheritance of a new shame-free life.

TINA'S STORY

I recall one evening at one of our women's gatherings how excited I was to teach about the gift of righteousness because I had finally had a breakthrough myself, and I was bubbling with joy. I remember my friend desperately desiring to have a revelation of Romans 5:17: "For if, by the trespass of the one man, death reigned through that one man, how much more will those who receive God's abundant provision of grace and the gift of righteousness reign in life through the one man, Jesus Christ!"

In tears, she confessed that she too had been a Christian for years yet never felt good enough, accepted, or approved of by God due to the legalistic teaching she heard and believed growing up. Tina believed some of her sins were just not forgivable. We prayed together and asked God to give her a deep understanding of Romans 5:17. To tell you the truth, I thought, *Well, it might take lots of studying scripture and time, but I pray she gets it at some point.* Ha ha! Great faith on my part!

The next morning she called me and said that she was awakened in the middle of the night and began to pray. She sensed that God told her to look at Galatians 5:22 which lists the fruit of the Spirit. That verse spoke so clearly to her: "Tina, it is My love, My joy, My peace, My self-control, and so on, that is in you. I'm in you! You focus on the gift I gave you and it will effortlessly flow from you. Stop trying to be 'good enough,' and just receive the gift I died for you to have."

It clicked for Tina. Realizing it wasn't her effort but His free gift of grace, she then was able to receive His righteousness, and her Shame Cloud dissipated. God saw her desire to live in the freedom He died for us to have and gently spoke to her that evening. She began walking in her "double portion" and inheritance.

 "Knock and the door shall open" (Matt. 7:7).

In story after story, "everlasting joy became ours" and more and more Shame Clouds dissolved when, like Tina, we openly confessed our need for help in receiving His "free gift of righteousness" (Rom. 5:17).

A common symptom of shame-based people is not believing they are worthy to receive forgiveness, that their offense is too great to be forgiven. Again, no surprise to God. Christ was bludgeoned for our shame. If we are honest with ourselves, we are being self-centered when we don't accept the gift of righteousness Jesus provided for us through His death on the Cross. We can be so self-focused and wallow in shame believing that *we* can actually do something for God to accept us or forgive us, OR, by faith, we can receive the gift Christ died for us to receive—*His life, His righteousness.* "I set before you life and death... choose life" (Deut. 30:15)!

MELANIE'S STORY

Melanie was raised Catholic and was educated for grades 1-12 in Catholic schools. One night, after a women's gathering where we studied our identity in Christ, Melanie left the group light-hearted and elated. She'd heard the Good News that she was made righteous when she became a follower of Christ and that she didn't need to earn that righteousness. She was experiencing the "everlasting joy," understanding that righteousness in Christ was a gift and that it was deposited inside of her, in her spirit. She had believed the "Fake News" (not the Good News) that she wasn't ever good enough and had to try hard each day to earn God's approval. Big voluminous Shame Clouds hovered over her throughout her youth and adult years, as she frequently sought approval and acceptance from others or her vocation. It was a heavy burden. The Shame Clouds evaporated with the revelation that Jesus took her shame at the Cross and exchanged it with forgiveness and righteousness. Melanie said that she had a new confidence and peace when she understood that she received the gift of righteousness when she accepted Christ. It was good news to Melanie to understand that her righteousness in Christ was constant and it didn't change if she sinned. She was always accepted and loved by God, and she was made righteous in her spirit when she was born again. "Come to Me all who labor and I will give you rest" (Matt. 11:28).

RENEW OUR MINDS TO THE TRUTH AND LIVE SHAME FREE!

To live shame-free we must renew our minds to the truth (Rom. 12:2) that GOD ISN'T MAD AT US! He is, however, MAD-LY in love with us. He doesn't see us in our sin. "He who knew no sin became sin so that we might become the righteousness of God in Jesus Christ" (2 Cor. 5:21). Jesus took all our sins, the sin of the world—and bore it in His body so that we could live in a relationship with God shame-free. Living in a healthy relationship with God is when we don't haul around that heavy feeling of shame when we sin or do something improperly.

When we live in shame we are basically saying that what Jesus did on the Cross wasn't good enough to remove our sin and guilt, so we have to punish ourselves and feel bad about who we are for the sins we have committed.

Feeling unworthy to receive is a symptom of a shame-based person. It baffles our human minds that someone sinless would take our guilt and punishment for something we did. So we shame ourselves. It's human nature. Do something wrong? The wrong must be punished. Then, from our anger and frustration of missing the mark, we shame others because we feel bad about ourselves.

Think of the mother who, in speaking to her child, finds the very same critical words coming out of her mouth that her mother used to say to her. It started generations ago, and it continues until we understand the true gospel and renew our minds to the truth that God took our shame by placing it on His Son. He is pleased with you because He sees Jesus in you. The more we stop focusing on our sins, the less we will sin. The more we focus on the *good news* that we were made righteous in Christ, the more we will live shame-free. We live out what we believe. Believing that we are now righteous in Christ and NOT "sinners saved by grace" (not even biblical) but saints who sin occasionally can help us beat a cycle of sin! It is a love response from us to Him when we focus on what He did for us on the Cross. We desire to love back, through obedience to His ways, when we understand the great love He demonstrated for us on the Cross. "For as a man thinks in his heart so it is" (Prov. 23:7, KJV).

THE SCAPEGOAT

In Leviticus 16, Aaron, the high priest at that time, prepared the physical sacrifice for the Yom Kippur celebration. He washed in pure water and clothed himself in pure white linen on the morning of the sacrifice. Two young goats and one bull were brought to him for the sacrifice offering. One goat and one bull were used for the sacrificial blood offering. One goat was used as a *scapegoat*. The blood of one of the goats and the bull were brought together into the center, the most holy place of the temple. That blood sacrifice atoned for the high priest, the Israelites, and the sanctuary. Then the stage was set for the live goat, the scapegoat. Aaron placed both hands upon the head of the goat and confessed aloud the sins of the nation, transferring them to the living goat. The sins and iniquities of the people carried over onto the goat's head. The scapegoat was then taken into the wilderness to prevent it from returning, getting the sin out of the camp so to speak. The sins of the Israelites were then atoned for one year.

A dramatic ancient tradition foreshadowing our Jesus, "the one who knew no sin but became sin so that we might become the righteousness of Jesus Christ" (2 Cor. 5:21). Shedding His blood and taking our sins, His body was broken for ours—Jesus, humbling Himself and becoming the *scapegoat*. Actually, He *is* the G.O.A.T! (Greatest Of All Time) "Blessed are those whose transgressions are forgiven, whose sins are covered. Blessed is the one whose sins the Lord will never count against them" (Rom. 4:7).

WHAT I'M GLAD I LEARNED

> "Instead of your shame, you will receive a double portion, and instead of disgrace, you will rejoice in your inheritance. And so you will inherit a double portion in your land, and everlasting joy will be yours" (Isa. 61:7).

I'm glad I learned that God's provision removed my shame and His heart is *for* us. I no longer have to hover under the weight of Shame Clouds. Renewing my mind daily to the truth of my new identity in Christ is the way to "possess a double portion in our land." I'm glad I learned that I am a child of the Most High God. That my Heavenly Father is pleased with me because He relates to me as His forgiven child—approved and accepted in His eyes.

Selah

WHAT ARE YOU THINKING ON?

Hebrews 10:17 states that He remembers our sin NO MORE. It is finished!

So why are you remembering your failures each day as a Born-Again Righteous Child of God with a New Identity? Are you carrying shame that is not yours to carry?

Below are just a few symptoms of shame-based people. Prayerfully consider if you find some of these operating in you.

- Having an "It isn't nice of me to take when I'm not giving" mentality
- Putting my needs last
- Difficulty receiving because I feel I'm not worthy
- Believing "I am bad, weak, stupid, undeserving"
- A compulsion to rescue others who are needy and disadvantaged
- Having one or more active addictions to substances, activities, unhealthy relationships
- Excessive sensitivity and defensiveness to perceived criticism or rejection
- Often misperceiving neutral feedback as criticism and/or wrongly assuming unspoken criticisms
- Habitual self-centeredness
- Constant belittling and discounting others while self-critical as well
- Excessive fault-finding
- Deflecting, discounting, or rejecting deserved compliments
- Chronically giving time and energy to others and getting little or nothing in return
- Repeatedly choosing, justifying, and tolerating relationships, situations, and/or environments that promote major shame

- Frequently choosing long-suffering, victim, saint, or martyr roles in key relationships and social settings without questioning why
- Being unable to do this self-love exercise

Chapter 3
I DIDN'T LEARN I HAVE A NEW IDENTITY IN CHRIST

66 "Therefore, if anyone is in Christ, the new creation has come. The old has gone, the new is here" (2 Cor. 5:17).

MY STORY

I remember teachings about "your identity in Christ." I acted like I understood what "identity in Christ" meant because I assumed if I were a Christian then it was a reference I should know and understand, but I didn't. It was like hearing the theological term "Eschatology" and thinking, *I'm a Christian, so I should know what that means. Hmmm?*

Identity is defined as who you are, the way you think about yourself, the way the world views you, and the characteristics that define you.

Understanding that I became a new creation in Christ and received a new identity was a foreign concept to me. What did this mean? My curiosity became fervent in discovering and understanding 2 Corinthians 5:17. How was I now a new creation, and where did the old creation go? What is new? What did becoming a "new creation" mean for me as a believer in Christ? If indeed I became a new creation then I must have a new identity too. What did that new identity look like?

I later discovered that having a deep understanding of who I am in Christ, the way I think about myself in Christ, and the characteristics I now have in Christ led me toward victorious living as a believer. And yet, I and many others didn't learn this in church. Knowing our new identity in Christ is to know a basic fundamental truth to a Christian's belief system. It's life-transforming and essential in our Christian walk. In John 8:32 it states "the truth that you **know** will set you free." Let's examine the fundamentals. When I became born again at the age of five there was a place inside of me that actually became brand new. I didn't know that at that time. I didn't know that for a really long time! All I knew was that I wasn't going to hell! Scripture says in 1 John 4:13, "We know that we live in Him and He in us because He has given us of His Spirit."

WE'VE GOT SPIRIT, YES WE DO, WE'VE GOT SPIRIT, HOW 'BOUT YOU?

Have you ever really taken the time to dwell on the fact that if you are a born-again Christian there is a place in you that becomes brand new? A place where the Spirit of God makes His home? I didn't look new when I accepted Christ; I didn't instantly act new when I was born again. So where did this new creation take place? It took place in my **spirit**. I didn't even know I had a spirit! I Thessalonians 5:23 states that we are made up of three parts: spirit, soul, and body.

> Now may the God of peace Himself sanctify you entirely; and may your **spirit** and **soul** and **body** be preserved complete, without blame at the coming of our Lord Jesus Christ" (1 Thes. 5:23).

Colossians 1:27 states that Christ Himself is in me. A supernatural transformation took place inside me—a new identity was placed inside me when I accepted Christ. At that time, all the characteristics of Christ were placed in my spirit. His strength, His mind, His love, His patience, His power, His faith, His righteousness, etc... I didn't have to go try to *be* these things in my own efforts or *get* them. They are my inheritance. They are in every born-again believer right now.

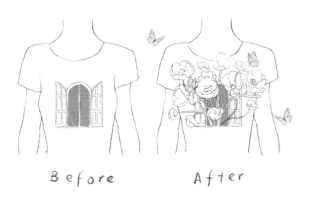

Before   After

SO WHAT?

Knowing that we have Christ's identity and characteristics inside of us enables every believer the opportunity to live the victorious life that God planned for us here on earth, not just when we get to Heaven.

Because we will live out what we believe or know to be true. "For as a man thinks, so he is" (Prov. 23:7).

For example, in my born-again spirit resides love, joy, peace, patience, long-suffering, kindness, goodness, faithfulness, gentleness, and self-control (Gal. 5:22). So when we cry out, "Oh, I need patience" when all the kids are crying and whining, when we are in traffic, or when someone at work is irritating us, we can dwell on the truth. The truth is that we already have patience dwelling inside us. We are equipped with every good thing in Christ because Christ is in us (Gal. 4:6). I have a better chance of behaving patiently because I know I already have it inside of me. For as a man thinks (he has patience), so he is (patient) (Prov. 23:7). What we think about ourselves becomes a reality. We will address that further in the chapter.

I can just imagine God saying with a smile, "Sweet child, why are you crying out to Me for patience? I gave it to you when you became a believer—it's already in you! Why are you asking for more faith? I deposited it in you already. Why are you begging for healing? I healed you at the Cross, and the same power that raised Jesus from the dead lives on the inside of you and gives life to your mortal body" (Rom. 8:11). (I can envision the hand-to-the-forehead emoji!) "Believe what I gave you, and think about that. Then you will see it manifest."

That's truth in action setting you free (John 8:32). It's a simple truth, but it isn't always simple...

> " The mind governed by the flesh is death, but the mind governed by the Spirit is life and peace (Rom. 8:6).

MY STORY—I'VE GOT SOUL

I get the lyrics to songs wrong. It's a running joke in our household and very entertaining to my kids. They often ask me, "Mom, what do you think they just said in that song?" I remember years ago having this conversation with a friend. She and I were laughing at what we thought certain lyrics were to songs from our youth. I admitted that I thought the song *Boogie Wonderland* by Earth, Wind, and Fire was, "You belong to Lance." Then she recollected that the Blues Brothers' song *Soul Man* was clearly saying, "I was so mad!" Can't you just hear John Belushi singing, "I'm a soul man," and my friend confidently belting out, "I was so mad!" She was confused.

I was confused too; I didn't know that I was more than a soul man! Our souls consist of our mind, will, and emotions. A good portion of my Christian life was led by my feelings. It was like riding a roller coaster up and down, fast, slow, and around the jerky bend. Peace, joy, and calm came when I learned the truth. God created us in three parts (1 Thes. 5:23). We've all heard the phrases: "He's your soulmate," "She's got soul," and "Let's win souls for Christ." But, I never focused on the truth that I was made of three parts— spirit, soul, and body. I just thought I was a "soul man."

So why does it matter?

We are a living testimony every day that the fruit of the Spirit **doesn't** reside in our souls. Our feelings, thoughts, and emotions can often be *the very opposite* of the good things deposited in our spirit. Living a Spirit-led life leads to peace and joy. Living life controlled by our feelings (our soul) often leads to inconsistency and confusion. We cannot rely on what we *feel*; we must rely on truth to experience victory. That's living by faith—believing what is true (God's Word) not being ruled by what we feel, taste, hear, smell, or see.

This is the Good News! We are new creations in Christ and God deposited every good thing in our spirits to live a life of freedom. We don't have to try to go get the fruit of the spirit. We already have it. This *is* "who we are in Christ"—the real you if you are a believer in Christ. And if we have these traits residing in us, then they can be activated in our lives. We can be ruled by the spirit and not the flesh (or soul). But, we must first renew our mind to the truth of who we are and what we have in Christ.

BUT I DON'T FEEL IT!

Many new Christians don't feel renewed. They walk around in condemnation still feeling guilt and shame because they are looking to see physical changes in their **body** or emotional changes in their **soul**. They fail to understand that we are made up of a third part, the **spirit.** *In accepting Christ's sacrifice, the primary shift occurs in our spirit.* But most of us only believe we are made up of a soul and body (without knowing that the spirit exists), so we don't recognize or walk in that change.

This is like wondering why a car with a functioning exterior (body) and engine (soul) won't drive but neglecting to remember that it has a gas tank that needs filling (spirit). The spirit gives life to the soul and body, and the soul and body reflect the change that happens in the spirit.

What is our body? Our physical **body** is made up of our skin, bones, organs, hair, etc. For example, when someone hugs us, we might feel the heat from them on our skin and the pressure of their touch on our physical body.

What is our soul? Our **soul** is made up of our mind, will, and emotions. For example, when someone hugs us, we might feel loved, happy, or even nervous emotions in our soul.

What is our spirit? Our **spirit** is the place where we became new and righteous. One can also say our spirit is where we are "born again." Before Christ, our spirit is empty and dead, but when we accept Christ our spirit becomes alive. Scripture tells us to worship God in spirit and in truth (John 4:24). It's where He equips us with every good thing to live a victorious life here on earth. Having a visual understanding that there is actually a place in us where we become a new creation and where Jesus's Spirit dwells confirms the statement:

"When God looks at you He sees Jesus."

I always thought when God looked at me He only saw my sin and mistakes. And that would be true if He related to me in the natural realm. I was never taught that God is Spirit (John 4:24) and He relates to the spirit part of me. The only reason God can have a relationship with me is that my spirit was renewed. God cannot be in a relationship with sin. So His Son, Jesus, took my sin and gave me His righteousness, and that took place in my spirit so that God could have a relationship with me. That's the Good News!

THE GOOD THINGS HE DEPOSITS IN EVERY BELIEVER

My born-again spirit is holy, perfect, righteous, doesn't sin, is sealed, constantly positive, and can't be penetrated by sin. It's greater than the world. It has the mind of Christ (1 Cor. 2:16). It has the faith of Christ. It has power. Not because of anything I did, but because of everything His Son did for me and deposited *into* my spirit. God equipped every believer with everything we need to live a victorious life here on earth through His Son Jesus. I have a new identity, and it isn't shameful. It is in Christ. I can confidently say I am the righteousness of God in Jesus Christ because of the exchange that took place in my born-again spirit.

So then why do I still fall short and sin? Usually, it's because I'm following my feelings or being ruled by my emotions. Every day I have to renew my mind to the truth of God's Word that tells me who I am and what I have in Christ. What I think affects my emotions and my behavior, therefore I will live out what I believe.

NANCY'S STORY

Years ago, Nancy prayed for more freedom in her daily spiritual life. She wanted to grow in experiencing His presence and intimate connection with Him as she moved through the day. She had been *doing* everything she thought she needed to *do*, but something was missing. Little did she know how God would answer that prayer.

He orchestrated our meeting through a very unusual set of circumstances that she knew could have only been divinely ordained. She joined three other ladies in our Bible study on the Holy Spirit. God soon developed a bond between the five of us which allowed us to share many prayers, laughs, and tears. We consequently named our group "The GGs" (Grace Girls).

Nancy learned how, as born-again Christians, the Spirit resides in us. He's pure and loving and when we let Him have control over governing our minds, it's powerful and peaceful. Nancy began to grow in living her life embracing this beautiful gift and thus lived more victoriously in His power. She found she had a choice to make throughout each day—whether she would let her mind be governed by the flesh or the Spirit. Once she understood that truth more deeply, her growth in godly power transformed her daily choices, actions, and thoughts, and she found indescribable freedom. She said, "Once I tasted its sweetness, it's simply alluring because it's God's Spirit... all things beautiful and free."

It was, of course, a process. And even though she understood it on a cognitive level, she sometimes reverted to living and thinking in the flesh, which left her feeling angst, conflicted, and unsettled, "like walking through my day wearing a pair of ill-fitting shoes," she shared. "Too small and painful. It hurts my heart because it's not the way I'm meant to live my life here on earth. Getting back to living in the Spirit is like shedding those ill-fitting shoes in favor of a perfectly fitting, cozy, soft pair of slippers... ahhh..."

God answered her prayer above and beyond what she could have ever anticipated *and* blessed her with deep relationships and lifelong friends in the process.

WHAT'S ON YOUR MIND?

Science supports these truths from scripture. What we believe or meditate on affects our choices and behavior and even our health. Dr. Caroline Leaf has worked in cognitive neuroscience for 25 years and pioneered work in neuroplasticity. She tells us, "The brain is like plastic and can be changed moment by moment through how we direct our thinking... in other words, the choices we make."

In her book *Switch on the Brain*, she shares scientific research to support that what we think on truly can affect our emotions, behavior, and health. She explains Epigenetics—the signals, including our thoughts, that affect the activity of our genes. What we think impacts our physical bodies.

> Be not conformed to this world, but be transformed by the renewing of your mind (Rom. 12:2).

Here are a few points I found helpful from her book:

Our minds are the most powerful thing God created. Science is recognizing the effect our thinking has on our bodies and brains. Science has proven that positive thinking changes the expression of our DNA and the way our genes convey themselves for the better.

We were created in God's image (Gen. 1:27). God designed us to be in agreement with Him and be like Him in our thinking. To set our minds on things above (Col. 3:2). His desire is for us to eliminate toxic thinking patterns that burden our minds and harm our bodies.

We are all made in His image and are designed for love not hate, bitterness, stress, and fear. When we operate in the opposite of how we were created it can cause dis-ease in our bodies.

He knew we would be challenged in our thinking and each night while we sleep baby nerve cells are born in our brains. This is called Neurogenesis. We have fresh cells in our brains each day to help us tear down toxic thoughts and reconstruct healthy thoughts. His mercies are new every morning (Lam. 3:23).

A VISION

I recall a time when the Lord was working with me on my thought life and the words I spoke over myself. I had never had a vision, but I read about several in scripture, and a handful of my brothers and sisters in Christ had shared visions they'd experienced with me. So, I was open to visions. But I think I told the Lord, "Just don't make them too weird." (I'm afraid I won't know what to do with a weird vision.) So, in His sweet patience with me, He gave me a picture of a bridal gown. It was a white, pristine, nipped-in-at-the-waist gown with full flowing white tulle on the bottom. The vision of that beautiful wedding gown invoked a response of *awe*. How beautiful! A response familiar to many of us when we see a beautiful bride walk down the aisle on her wedding day.

Then in my spirit, I sensed the Lord telling me, "That is how I see you." It was such a sweet, delightful, peaceful picture. He then said, "Now I want you to take a black Sharpie to that beautiful, expensive gown and write as many ugly words as you can think of. Then take a sharp razor and cut the tulle to shreds."

My response was, "I CAN'T DO THAT TO THAT BEAUTIFUL, EXPENSIVE GOWN!"

His response in my spirit was, "That's right, you can't, but you *do*. Every time you speak badly about yourself or negatively think of yourself, you shred and destroy My beautiful bride that I made. I paid a huge price for that bride and you destroy the gift I gave you every time you speak badly or think negatively about yourself—My bride."

That was so impactful to me. God gave us a new identity through His Son Jesus—an identity without blemish, like that white, pristine bridal gown. He calls us to think about everything that is lovely, perfect, and pure (Phil. 4:8). The gift of righteousness that Christ gave us at salvation is who we are in Christ. Our identity in Christ is lovely, perfect, and pure. The more we dwell on His gift of righteousness, the more it affects our emotions and behavior for the good.

Letting your sinful nature control your mind leads to death. But letting the Spirit control your mind leads to life and peace (Rom. 8:6).

A couple of years ago I spoke at a women's ministry gathering on our identity in Christ. At the end of the teaching, I put a beautiful white bridal gown on display. I asked a few volunteers to come up and write some negative thoughts they had about themselves on the gown with a black Sharpie. Of course, their first response was, "Oh no, I can't do that on this beautiful expensive gown." But, after some coaxing, several women wrote the messages that plagued their minds. "I'm not good enough," "I'm guilty," "I'm not smart," and the list goes on. Imagine their faces as I explained that they were writing on the very gown of the Bride of Christ—marring the image that He saw as so lovely and perfect.

Before   After

WHAT I'M GLAD I LEARNED

Knowing the truth of who I am in Christ and what I have in Christ transformed my daily living. It has allowed me to walk in victory daily because I'm not ruled by my emotions. My day, mood, and circumstances are no longer ruled by what I can see, taste, hear, and feel in the natural world. When I choose daily to think about everything that is lovely, pure, true, and perfect (Phil. 4:8), I reside in peace and joy even when I am going through a challenging situation because my mind is fixed on what is true. I invite you to dwell on the truth of all that God has given you and know that you can live in the daily freedom that He died for you to experience.

SELAH

So, what's on your mind?

What would you write on that gown?

What does God say about you?

Chapter 4
I DIDN'T LEARN I HAVE AN ENEMY

66 "The thief comes only to steal and kill and destroy: I came that they may have life, and have it abundantly" (John 10:10).

I like to read this particular Scripture like this..."I have come that they may have life, and have it abundantly. The thief comes only to steal and kill and destroy."

Why do I like to read and profess John 10:10 in this order? Focusing on the One who is greater reminds me that the battle was won and the thief has been defeated. I like to speak it out loud and meditate on the power of God's life in me, working through me. It also gives me hope and refocuses me when my circumstances are not looking or feeling so light-hearted or joyful.

We have an opponent.

The only knowledge I had of the devil growing up was a red figure holding a pitchfork who lived in hell. Was there really an evil principality roaming around seeking whom he could devour?

MY STORY

Growing up in a very conservative denomination I never heard any reference to Satan. Sadly, I didn't even know there was an enemy. For that matter, I never even knew that there was a spiritual realm outside of the natural realm we live in. I was "being destroyed for my lack of knowledge" (Hosea 4:6). What a great tool of the enemy to deceive believers, to tell them that there isn't an enemy out there to kill, steal, and destroy us. Then we believers don't have a clue how to fight the enemy *or that we are even in a battle.* Satan is now free to whisper lies into our ears—knowing that we'll believe the thoughts are ours and fall prey to self-condemnation, or even blame others—putting us all at odds. As I became awakened through the scripture about the enemy and his plan, I discovered this was the main reason Jesus came—to defeat the works of the enemy (1 John 3:8). How could one NOT teach about it? Or even mention it? Satan loves when God's people are deceived!

I recall even being too fearful to bring up the fact that I thought Satan was real amongst some of the churchgoers at my conservative denomination. I thought I would get kicked out of my church. How absurd! Thankfully, the Lord divinely connected me with a couple of friends who believed in the spiritual realm. They were able to teach me much about the enemy's tactics. The truths that they taught me were based on scripture, and those truths began to set me free.

The first truth was that one of the enemy's easiest access points is through our thoughts and our emotions. Scripture tells us to take every thought captive, to think on everything pure and lovely (Phil. 4:8). As I began to learn this truth, I started listening to my thoughts. What a crazy playground that was—HA! Were my thoughts lies from the enemy or were they true? Sometimes there may have been a little truth in what I was thinking, but mixed with a huge exaggeration or a negative thought that would instill fear or self-condemnation. It was like a record skipping and playing the same song over and over in my mind for years.

Here were some of the "The Enemy's Greatest Hits":

You're ugly.

They think you are stupid.

They are so much better than you.

You can't do that.

You aren't good enough.

They are mad at you.

And during my bouts with insomnia and postpartum depression:

You're not going to sleep tonight.

You're going to be on medicine for the rest of your life.

Your kids are going to be messed up.

You are going to die.

You are going to be hospitalized.

You are not saved.

Now that kind of thinking can make a person feel insane!

Dwelling on fearful thoughts for too long can greatly affect our emotions and steal our peace and joy. Toxic thinking can cause anxiety, stress, and lead to health problems—just the way Satan would love to have it. Thankfully, God gave us His Word to defeat the enemy. For every wrong thought, I had a verse memorized and ready to combat it. It took some time to develop new thinking patterns, but with some practice and consistency over the years, I have seen healthy thought patterns take hold. It also has been great healing to my body and peace in my everyday living.

We also have the promises of God's armor stated in Ephesians 6:10-16:

 Finally, be strong in the LORD and in His mighty power. Put on the full armor of God, so that you can take your stand against the devil's schemes. For our struggle is not against flesh and blood, but against the rulers, against the authorities, against the powers of this dark world and against the spiritual forces of evil in the heavenly realms. Therefore put on the full armor of God, so that when the day of evil comes, you may be able to stand your ground, and after you have done everything, to stand. Stand firm then, with the belt of truth buckled around your waist, with the breastplate of right-eousness in place, and with your feet fitted with the readiness that comes from the gospel of peace. In addition to all this, take up the shield of faith, with which you can extinguish all the flaming arrows of the evil one. Take the helmet of salvation and the sword of the Spirit, which is the word of God. And pray in the Spirit on all occasions with all kinds of prayers and requests. With this in mind, be alert and always keep on praying for all the LORD's people.

DEFEATING THE ENEMY

God's covering, protection, and provision were ever-present in the darkest time of my life. I battled postpartum depression, insomnia, and anxiety at levels deeper than ever before after the birth of our fifth child. Our family suffered through the pain of wondering if their mom and wife would ever be the same. *I* wondered if I would ever be the same. I questioned if living life in that state was worth living. I did continue to get healthy, however, it wasn't overnight. During that dark time, the Lord gave me a prophetic dream.

It was so vivid and tangible that I knew it was from the Lord. I saw a beautiful light reaching me and felt a deep love and peace that was indescribable—nothing like the love and peace and joy I had experienced in this world. I remember not wanting to leave His presence and thinking, *this has to be what Heaven must be like.* Suddenly, a dark female warrior stood at the side of my bed with arrows in her belt and ammunition of every kind secured in a military jacket she wore. It was daunting, but with the little strength I had, I got out of bed and stood up to the enemy, and she vanished. I believe God was showing me I had victory over the enemy in my current battle if I stood up and faced my enemy in God's strength. I also believe the Lord allowed me to see how my battle of depression would end in victory and that I would conquer it through Christ.

That visual was so important for me to remember because at that desperate time I could barely stand up. Only through His power could I stand and stand firmly. Thankfully, I had truth hidden in my heart, armed to defeat the enemy. I'm not sure if during that time I was wearing the breastplate of righteousness because it wasn't until I began to heal that I became aware of God's gift of righteousness. My "shoes of peace" were fitted on my feet as I trusted in God's peace. I took up my shield of faith and spoke the truth as much as I could when the enemy shot a lie or dart at me. Reminding myself of who I was in Christ was the helmet of salvation that covered my mind, and cutting the evil one's lies with God's truth enabled me to win the battle. God surrounded me with friends and family who also used all of their armor to stand in the gap and war for me through prayer and encouragement during those dark days.

It wasn't just friends and family that God used. He also used strangers, which I discovered on a visit to another doctor who practiced both conventional and functional medicine. My anxiety was so great it was difficult for me to focus. I hardly had any strength to drive to the appointment. Thankfully, a dear friend took me. The doctor suggested doing several hormone and chemical level tests. As I tearfully listened to her instructions, she paused our conversation and said, "I see this huge black cloud all around you and an army of evil soldiers trying to destroy you. You are going to defeat this army, and you are going to share a great testimony."

She then went on to share how she had gone through a great struggle when her husband came home one day and said he was leaving. Through the divorce, her children also left her. At that lowest point of her life, she turned to Christ and became a warrior for Him. Slowly, the Lord restored her relationship with her kids. He led her to get into medicine, which she now used to help others heal. One of her gifts was seeing into the spiritual realm. When I was first exposed to people who have that gift, it freaked me out. But what a gift it was to me at that time. What courage that doctor had to share it with me. It was truly a vision from God to encourage me to not give up and keep pressing in.

Verse 18 from Ephesians 6 says, "And pray in the Spirit on all occasions with all kinds of prayers and requests." Pray in the Spirit? For some reason, verse 18 was commonly overlooked when I heard this passage on the armor of God taught. It's clearly important if it says to do so on all occasions. This is another truth I didn't learn in church (more on that in chapter 5). I'll leave you one last testimony about the reality of the war we're in.

MY MOM'S STORY (Grandma got run over by her Lexus)

My mother tells a terrifying and revelatory tale here in her own words:

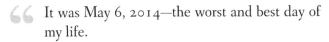 It was May 6, 2014—the worst and best day of my life.

At 11:30 at night, I left a Bible study at my son's house. Our study consisted of 10 women, and we always had such a good time that our study would often last four hours! (I never dreamed I could enjoy a Bible study for four hours.) I walked the long distance from the porch to my car, got in, turned on the ignition, and started down the driveway. I heard flower pots rattling in the back seat, so I thought I'd better stop and rearrange the pots so they wouldn't break. I put my car in park (or so I thought), and got out of the car. When I reached the back door, I realized my car was moving backward towards me. I hadn't put the gear completely in park, and it slipped into reverse.

45

As I saw the car moving towards me, I knew it could hit three other cars in the driveway, so I tried to jump into the front seat, put my foot on the brake, and stop the car (just like I'd seen in the movies). Well, I didn't make it. I got as far as grabbing the steering wheel, was caught off balance, and fell backward onto the driveway with my head towards the back of the car. I thought I was safe because I was parallel to the vehicle. But I didn't realize that by grabbing the steering wheel, I had slightly changed the direction the car was heading. My eyes were closed; I heard a crunching sound and thought that the car had run over a cellophane wrapper and bumped my foot. I felt no pain. I then realized that the car might run over my head. Surely not—this can't be happening! I was terrified and cried out, "Oh God, don't let this car go over my head!" Then I saw my words ascending towards the sky. At this moment, an amazing peace came over me. I thought, *How can I be so peaceful and calm in this situation?* But the more I prayed, the more peaceful I became. In fact, it felt so wonderful that I said to God, "If you want to take me now, I'm ready to go."

I felt so fantastic that I actually wanted to be with Him. Although I knew Jesus Christ as my personal Savior, I had always been a little afraid of dying. Next, I saw a piece of mauve-colored fabric off to the right—was it a rug, a towel, a blanket? What was it and why was it there? Then a beautiful, blue sky appeared with a silvery light shining through a very thin veil. I found myself smiling. I knew without a doubt that God was there with me. I was actually getting excited. Do I dare talk to Him? Well, after all, He's my Father, and I'm His child. At this point, what have I got to lose? I remember saying, "God, I want to see your face —can I?"

He said in a very authoritative voice, "No one is allowed to see my face." I said, "That's okay, I understand." Then a few silvery beams appeared as if He was saying, "I will only show you a small part of Me." I was smiling and somehow I knew that He was smiling too. I was certain I was in the presence of God the Almighty, the Creator of the world, the Creator of the moon, stars, snowflakes and snails, black holes and galaxies, the ants and elephants. Yet there He was with me—regular Ruth Rogers. What an extraordinary privilege! I thought, *maybe He makes Himself known to everyone when they are about to die.*

Next, a thin black veil appeared in front of a milky-white translucent wall, and toward it zoomed a dark, ominous figure, which hit the wall, veered off, and was gone. It really scared me. Was that the enemy, the prince of darkness, an angel of death? But immediately I also sensed a magnificence and power like I'd never known, and I knew that it was God. He was there too, and I felt so safe.

Then nothing happened. Could the car have possibly passed me by? At that instant, I saw the fabric (that "blanket of protection") zip towards me and cover my head. Then I felt the rubber from the tire hit the right side of my forehead. I knew the "blanket" was there, even though I couldn't feel it. But I *did* feel the tire cross my forehead. There was lots of pressure but no pain. When the tire reached the left side above my eye, I felt the pressure increase so much that I thought my head was going to split open and that my life was over. I felt excruciating sharp pain for only a split second, but then it disappeared. I found myself smiling and thinking, *I'm in the midst of a miracle.*

I heard the engine pass. I was still alive! I was smiling—it was so hard to believe that I was happy! Then I thought, *Maybe this is how Christian martyrs feel when they are about to suffer a horrific death.* The Bible tells the story of Stephen singing while he was being stoned. Perhaps God gives martyrs a wonderful sense of protection, peace, and comfort, and they cannot feel the pain. I would hope so.

I stood up and was so dizzy that I fell over, landed on my left side, then rolled over to my stomach and down a small embankment. I heard the car coming behind me. I spotted an evergreen and grabbed the bottom branch, heard the car less than a foot away on my left side, and watched as it passed me by. It hit the tree that I was holding on to and uprooted it. The roots of the tree being torn from the ground sounded like thunder. God had protected me again. "Thank you, Lord, for letting me live. Now what should I do? Please help me, God." I started screaming for someone in the house to come and help me, but no one came. I got up—surprised that I could walk. I started back towards the porch, but I felt so nauseated and weak.

Finally, the women in the house heard me screaming and came to my rescue. The next thing I knew I was in the ambulance. The first thing I said to the attendant was, "Please check my head because the car ran over my forehead."

He turned to his partner and laughed and said, "She thinks the car ran over her head." I could understand his reaction and skepticism. What if I told him the rest of the story?

Despite everything that happened, I was extremely fortunate to end up with only a broken small toe, fractured foot, and hematoma on my thigh. But the flower pots never broke!

Ephesians 6:12 says, "Our struggle is not against flesh and blood, but against the rulers, against the authorities, against the powers of this dark world, and against the spiritual forces of evil in the heavenly realms." I saw that firsthand.

I always knew there were principalities operating in the world, but trust me, I had *never* witnessed them at work with my own eyes. If someone had told me this story, I would've probably rolled my eyes and said, "Yeah, yeah."

However, when I first got out of the car to move the flower pots, I saw what I believe were demons in front of the car—huge worm-like creatures with no eyes or heads, rusty red in color, and crawling over each other. On the lawn, I saw a circle of sheer white ghost-like figures, each about 10 feet in length moving very rapidly. *What in the world is that?!* I thought. I knew I was in the presence of something very evil. We need to be watchful and prepared.

Yes, the accident was a horrendous experience, but it was also the best thing I ever experienced in my life. Having such a real encounter with God Almighty was a wonderful gift that has strengthened and impacted my walk with Him.

WHAT I'M GLAD I LEARNED

I'm so very thankful that I can stand on the truth that the enemy has been defeated by Christ's power and resurrection. That I have learned to think about and speak God's truth over the enemy's attacks and lies. That I need to be alert and stay well balanced as stated in 1 Peter 5:8 because there really is an enemy seeking to seize upon our lives. That he is a defeated foe and that through Christ I have victory to combat his attempts to try to kill, steal, and destroy all things!

SELAH

Do you believe an enemy is trying to steal from you, and even kill and destroy you?

What lies can you identify that may be a repeated pattern in your thought life?

Do you believe Christ came to give you life and victory—to overcome the lies of the enemy?

What truths do you use to replace the lies?

Chapter 5
I DIDN'T LEARN THE POWER OF THE HOLY SPIRIT

My friend and I stood in her kitchen, as we did many afternoons with our young toddlers, sharing about our daily activities and discussing many topics. I finally got the courage to ask about this "other baptism." I was somewhat apprehensive to bring it up for fear that a "good Christian" should know about it. The only baptism I was familiar with was water baptism. As our sweet Lord would have it, my friend went on to explain to me that in her youth she had attended a church that taught and believed in the baptism of the Holy Spirit. That she had been baptized with the Holy Spirit and prayed in tongues.

I was relieved I had a friend who was familiar with this baptism and yet scared at the same time because only "weird" Christians prayed in tongues, and I was concerned that I would get kicked out of my church if I did the same. However, the Holy Spirit was nudging me to search this matter out.

I then asked my spiritual mentor Arline about this baptism. I trusted Arline. She had grown up in a conservative denomination, was an elder, and was wise. She couldn't be *wacky*?! Arline shared with me about the baptism of the Holy Spirit and praying in tongues and that a prayer language is available to all believers. She explained that it was a prayer language that the enemy couldn't understand. It was given to edify, encourage, and strengthen the believer. She directed me to 1 Corinthians 12 to learn more about it, and then she invited me to be baptized in the Holy Spirit.

I remember being so timid. Every fearful thought went through my mind about receiving this baptism and praying in tongues. I could see it now: my husband would think I'm a freak, my parents would agree with my husband, and then I'd get kicked out of my church!

I prayed and asked the Lord, "If you want me to be baptized in the Holy Spirit, then orchestrate it." Soon after, Arline invited me to her condo in downtown Chicago to receive the baptism of the Holy Spirit. She said that I could come over and that she and her husband, Fred, would explain it to me and lay hands on me. I agreed, but inside I was thinking it was a bit weird. In fact, I was trying to figure out how I could get out of that commitment.

I prayed, "Lord, I will only do this and know that it is you if there is a parking space right in front of her building." (For sure that would be an out because there were *never* parking spaces in front of Arline's building in downtown Chicago. That would be a miracle in itself!) I pulled up, and right in front of Arline's building was a big, wide-open parking space!

I arrived at Arline's apartment and she said, "Hopefully Fred will get home and we can pray with you." I admit I was praying that Fred wouldn't make it home. I had to get back to the suburbs to relieve a babysitter, so I was watching the clock closely and was just about to grab my coat to leave when who walks in the door, but Fred! "Oh, praise the Lord," said Arline (I was not thinking the same). Fred and Arline prayed over me and began to do so in their prayer language. It was beautiful and I was moved to tears but didn't pray in tongues myself at that time. I was too intimidated. I needed to learn more about this.

I studied the scriptures, prayed, and then called my sister-in-law and told her about my experience. Several months later my sister-in-law called me after going to a Christian conference and said, "I got the tongues!"

I exclaimed, "NO WAY! You just went down and got baptized in the Holy Spirit and began praying in tongues?"

She said, "Yes!" That's what I love about my sister-in-law. She is always full of courage and just goes for it.

That's all I needed. I hung up the phone and said, "In the name of competition, I can do this!" HA! Then I simply began to pray in a prayer language. It was so sweet and full of His loving presence. It made my faith graduate to another level. And it confirmed to me that the Holy Spirit was living inside of me.

BAPTISM IN THE HOLY SPIRT AND PRAYER LANGUAGE

As we look at the scriptures, it is very clear that there was a second baptism (Matthew 3:11, Acts 1:8, Mark 1:8, Luke 3:16, John 1:33). John the Baptist talks about Jesus coming to baptize in the Holy Spirit in all four Gospels. So why is this such a contested issue and one which many churches don't even discuss? Maybe some churches are afraid of the power of the Holy Spirit and the supernatural gifts that come with the Baptism in the Holy Spirit. Yet, throughout the Gospels, there is a clear pattern of Jesus baptizing disciples in the Holy Spirit. Jesus Himself was baptized in the Holy Spirit (Luke 3:22). So my question is: if Jesus was into it, what is there to be afraid of? More importantly, why wouldn't you want it? I also believe some churches believe the prayer language that usually accompanies the Baptism in the Holy Spirit seems weird, abnormal, and even demonic. So better to ignore this baptism or gift of tongues than seem weird?

Baptism in the Holy Spirit is the power that enables the believer to walk out their salvation. A prayer language is a powerful gift because it is a perfect prayer by the Holy Spirit (Rom. 8:26-27). Our own prayers are important, but also flawed, full of our own imperfect perceptions and motivations. God wants to hear them—they are a vital part of our relationship with Him. But when we pray in the Holy Spirit, the all-knowing and perfect Spirit of God interacts with our spirits and speaks directly to God on our behalf—praying in ways we are too limited to pray on our own. It is powerful because satan can't understand our prayer language. It is a heavenly language. If the enemy can't understand it, then he is left in the dark about our communication with God. A prayer language also edifies, encourages, and gives power to the believer (Jude 1:20). Don't we all need edification and encouragement and power? Maybe that's why at the end of Ephesians 6 Paul says "to pray in the Spirit on ALL occasions."

The enemy's best strategy is to lie to Christians and say things like, "This was only for the early disciples and not for today," "Not everyone can pray in tongues," and "You will be a freak if you do." NONSENSE! Over the past 20 years, every person that I have been in fellowship with, from ages

20-80, who is thirsting for more of the Lord, received the baptism in the Holy Spirit and received their prayer language. Some prayed in tongues right away and some prayed later.

I often feel skeptical that my own family will not be open to receiving "suggestions or ideas" from me regarding faith issues. I worry that they'll say, "Oh, there goes Mom on another one of her teachings." However, they were open when I talked to them about baptism in the Holy Spirit, and each received their prayer language. They simply came with "child-like" faith ready to receive from God. It's comforting to know my children and husband now have a prayer language that the enemy cannot understand and a gift that is available to them at all times to encourage, edify, and strengthen them. Maybe that is why Paul said, "I thank God that I speak in tongues more than all of you" (1 Cor. 14:18). Some may think, *Dang Paul, you don't mind bragging*, but maybe he was saying, "I pray in the Spirit more than ever because it isn't my mind or ideas; it's the Holy Spirit praying God's perfect will through me. It strengthens me, encourages me, and equips me to serve Him and to do what God has called me to do."

KATIE'S STORY

Katie was one of the OG's in the first family room gathering 25 years ago. She was invited by a friend and accepted Christ after attending some of our Bible studies. About five years ago, we gathered in Chicago to do a study on the Holy Spirit and the baptism in the Holy Spirit. Seeing that most of the women grew up in very conservative denominations I wasn't sure what the women would think about baptism in the Holy Spirit or praying in tongues. Katie was always introspective and had a quiet demeanor during our studies. One afternoon after Bible Study, Katie and I went to lunch and she shared that she was determined to get her prayer language. She was driving in her car and asked the Lord to baptize her in the Holy Spirit and she started to pray in her prayer language. I was so surprised by Katie's determination to receive what God had for her. Katie was transformed again by God's gift of the Holy Spirit.

Praying in the Spirit is Romans 8:26-28 in action:

> *In the same way, the Spirit helps us in our weakness. We do not know what we ought to pray for, but the Spirit himself intercedes for us through wordless groans. And he who searches our hearts knows the mind of the Spirit, because the Spirit intercedes for God's people in accordance with the will of God.*

Learning how to pray in the Spirit was a relief for me. I often don't know the exact words to pray, and when I do find the words, I often pray with an agenda of my own. I want to pray for and about these issues and people, but not according to my understanding.

When praying in the Spirit, I can be praying about the deep concerns of my heart, yet it's aligned with the Lord's will. The Holy Spirit is helping me in my weakness, interceding on my behalf, knowing the concerns of my heart, and aligning my prayers with the will of God. That's amazing.

STEPHANIE'S STORY

About 10 years ago, Stephanie was invited by a friend to my mom's family room where we were studying how to hear from God. We also talked about the baptism of the Holy Spirit and praying in tongues. Stephanie could easily relate, having been raised in a charismatic background. This is her story:

> "Just close your eyes, lift your hands, and speak the name of Jesus," she said. I was 13 years old, worshiping and praying at the altar during an evening service at church camp. That was the day I received my prayer language. I was fortunate to have been raised in a home and church that spoke about and encouraged receiving the gift of the Holy Spirit and speaking in tongues.
>
> I remember an elder in the church, Sister Nell, who had the gift to translate a prophetic word given in tongues. Sometimes during an intense period of worship, someone would share a word from the Lord. Our pastor would instruct us to be still and pray and listen. He said the Lord would provide someone to interpret the word. I remember as a child feeling nervous, thinking... *But what if no one here can translate what was said?* I began to learn, fortunately, if the Lord has a prophetic word to share, He will provide a witness to discern. Sometimes Sister Nell would stand up boldly at her pew, speak in tongues in a loud voice to the congregation, and then pause for a moment before sharing what the Lord had revealed to her. I discovered later that the prophetic word spoken almost always had been scripture from the Bible, although I don't recall anyone reciting a book, chapter, and verse after sharing.

As a child, I vividly recollect hearing my mother spending time with the Lord. She often prayed aloud, and it was common for her to begin speaking in her prayer language. This made me curious about speaking in tongues. I wondered if it was only to share a word from the Lord or if some would only speak in tongues privately. I came to learn that there are different types of this gift. Although we should seek and desire the gift of speaking in tongues in all forms, we may not have the prophetic gift of translation. I understood, though, that the gift of speaking in tongues is available to all believers. It was something I desired in my life from a young age. I had been taught that the Lord would give me His words when I didn't know what or how to pray.

This brings me back to that special night at church camp... The pastor had instructed us to seek and ask the Lord to give us this gift of speaking in tongues. I stood at that altar with my arms raised high. It seemed like a long time. My arms grew heavy and tired. I kept praying and asking though. I remember worshiping the Lord and telling Him how I loved, adored, and praised Him. All at once, I felt a chill, like a shiver, all over. It washed over my entire body, like a warm, shimmery feeling under my skin. It went from my head to my toes. I began to say words that I didn't understand, but I felt such a love and connection with Christ. Tears came to my eyes. It seemed I prayed for more than an hour at the altar that evening. I didn't want to leave.

It has been like that ever since, whenever I spend time communing with the Lord in my prayer language. For some reason, it's easier for me to enter into speaking in tongues after I've been worshiping and earnestly seeking the Lord. I often open my hands, palms up, and speak aloud words like, "Holy Spirit, come. I welcome you." Speaking in my prayer language is always more effective when I audibly speak, although sometimes I pray in my prayer language quietly in a whisper. I don't always know what I'm praying. Sometimes the Lord will give me an understanding of it. There have been seasons of my life when I've been distant from the Lord, but as soon as I come back and reestablish my commitment, I've always been able to find my prayer language again.

As an adult, I was extremely fortunate to become part of a small group of women who study the Bible and pray together—an edifying part of my spiritual growth. I'm grateful this group allows time and space for us to welcome the Holy Spirit into our lives. In our culture, it seems there aren't enough welcoming places that encourage communing with the Lord this way. As I've grown spiritually, I realize how important it is to regularly connect with the Father speaking in my prayer language. It strengthens my spirit and grounds me more deeply in my personal relationship with Him.

THEY JUST WANTED MORE

A couple of my friends were in their quiet time fellowship-ping with the Lord. They said, "I want more of you," and began praying in tongues. They were open and desired more of the Father—not just trying to have an experience. It isn't a language that just starts pouring out of you that you can't control. It's just like talking. You can talk when and if you want. One of my friends who was coming out of the gay lifestyle shared with me that he had just become a Christian and was crying out to the Lord for help asking, "How am I going to leave this lifestyle?" As he was lying down one evening praying, he began to speak in his prayer language for the first time. He knew it was a powerful gift given to strengthen him to move out of that dark place. Today I see so many believers limping along, not empowered to move forward. The believers back in Jesus's day were empowered because, after salvation, it was the norm to receive the baptism of the Holy Spirit. As we read in Acts 10, it was just part of the package.

THE HOLY SPIRIT HIT HAITI

On a mission trip to Haiti a few years ago, the pastors of a couple of churches had been teaching about the Holy Spirit. How beautiful it was to see the believers from those churches so eager to grow in their faith. They walked miles to hear their pastors teach the Word and to fellowship with each other for hours at a time. No one was looking at their watches after three worship songs and a forty-five-minute teaching. They were full of joy, worshiping for hours and hearing God's Word. Our team had the honor of laying hands on well over 200 believers and witnessing them receive their prayer language. They came expecting and ready to receive what the Lord had for them. We left thanking God that they had a powerful prayer language that would build them up, which Satan couldn't understand, and a language that prayed God's perfect prayer. Their spiritual hunger was met with a great gift!

The enemy has deceived too many believers into thinking that baptism of the Holy Spirit and praying in tongues isn't for everyone in the body today and that it was only for the believers in the book of Acts.

I have witnessed the opposite. I have seen believers' relationships with the Lord deepen and strengthen to new levels as they began "praying in the Spirit on all occasions." A friend of mine explained it this way: "Imagine a Christmas tree in the corner of the family room beautifully decorated with lights twinkling, and there are several gorgeously-wrapped gifts with big, vibrant bows resting under the tree. They are all for you. You just have to go over and take one, receive it, and open it."

WHAT I'M GLAD I LEARNED

I am very thankful the Lord taught me about the baptism of the Holy Spirit and the gift of praying in tongues. It has strengthened me daily, guided me in decisions, rejuvenated me, and given me courage outside of myself to help others. It gives me discernment when I don't know what to pray. It calms my emotions and gives me peace as I trust that God's perfect will is being communicated (and not my own) when I pray in the Spirit on all occasions (Eph. 6:18).

SELAH

Do you believe there is more than water baptism?

Do you desire to receive the baptism of the Holy Spirit and a prayer language?

Do you believe that God desires to empower all believers with a prayer language?

Luke 11:13: "If you then, though you are evil, know how to give good gifts to your children, how much more will your Father in Heaven give the Holy Spirit to those who ask Him!" —Jesus

Prayer for Baptism in the Holy Spirit

"Do not leave Jerusalem, but wait for the gift my Father promised, which you have heard me speak about. For John baptized with water, but in a few days you will be baptized with the Holy Spirit" (Acts 1:4-5).

> *Father God, I thank You that I have had the indwelling of Your Holy Spirit when I accepted Christ at salvation. I ask You now to immerse me in Your Holy Spirit and give me the gift of a prayer language. Thank You for giving me this free gift; I receive it by faith.*

PRACTICAL TIPS WHEN BEGINNING TO PRAY IN TONGUES:

Remember that the language doesn't just jump out of you unexpectedly. You have control over when you speak. I like Robert Morris' teaching, "The God I Never Knew." He says you have control over when you speak in tongues. It's not going to hit you while you are grocery shopping, where all of a sudden you get this urge to start praying in your prayer language over the intercom. You can turn it on and off just like you do with your own human language.

It may sound like gibberish at first, but so does a baby when he or she begins to speak.

A friend of mine said she got into the shower and played worship music and began to praise God. The sound of the shower and music helped her get her mind off of what she was saying, and then the language just began to flow.

PRIMING THE PUMP!

Many times, when I have been in groups that have been baptized in the Spirit, we have one person pray aloud in their prayer language, then ask the person who was recently baptized to repeat what words or phrases they hear in the other person's prayer language. It's sort of like "priming the pump." Then after a few minutes, the person will inevitably start praying in their own language, not repeating the other person at all. This has always been helpful and effective because it is all new, and many people wonder what it sounds like and how to get the language to flow.

Lastly, like anything new, it takes practice. You may think you are saying the same thing over and over, but keep practicing and your vocabulary will increase. Don't doubt that it isn't your prayer language. Satan would love for you to doubt because he can't understand it and it is a powerful gift—a gift he certainly doesn't want you to receive.

Chapter 6

I DIDN'T LEARN THAT THE BIBLE IS RELEVANT, ESSENTIAL, & POWERFUL

The Bible - Relatable for Today?

Twenty-five years ago when 10 of us gathered in a living room to study God's Word, we had no idea the Bible was so relatable or powerful. The misconception most of us would have said we'd believed was that the Bible was only for theologians and pastors to read on Sunday. We were real, everyday women desiring to learn how God's Word was relevant for today. A few things we learned together about God's Word—The Bible: It is relevant, valuable, reliable, powerful, and essential.

Scripture tells us God's instructions and promises are to be desired more than gold (Ps. 19:10).

It must be valuable. It is the most purchased book in history. It hits the best-seller list every year, but sadly it isn't even listed anymore because it would be monotonous to state the same best-seller every year. It is also the most shoplifted book in the world. It must be essential!

What makes it so valuable? I recall asking my daughter at a young age why she thought the Bible was so valuable and essential. Her response was so straight forward:

"Mom, it's the Word of God!" (like, duh!)

GOD SPEAKING TO US

Don't we all long to hear and know the Word of God? To know and understand the Creator of the Universe's thoughts? God, show me which way to turn. God, do you really heal today? God, do I have a purpose? God, will you restore my family? God, are you there? God, will you really provide for all my needs? God, do you care? God, do you love me? God, do you really forgive me for *that*?

"In the beginning was the Word and the Word was with God, and the Word was God Himself" (John 1:1).

God's thoughts, or in the Greek "logos," are available to us 24/7 to meditate on, feast on, and digest. All-knowing God leaves us with His instructions, promises, prophecies, and parables.

But, is it **reliable**? With over 24,000 New Testament manuscripts discovered to date, the Bible stands as the best-preserved ancient literary work. Compare this with the second-best-preserved literary work of antiquity, Homer's *Iliad*, with only 643 preserved manuscripts thus far. The works of Herodotus and Thucydides with only eight preserved manuscripts, Caesar's *Gallic War* has 9-10, and Livy's *Roman History* has 20.

I'd say expert historians on ancient manuscripts have great evidence that the Bible is reliable.

MY STORY

I never knew that the Bible could be so relatable or powerful. I never knew you didn't have to have a degree in theology to study it. I was struck by the peace myself and the women in the group experienced when we began to study together and become familiar with God's promises in the Bible. It was truly relevant to many of our circumstances. It wasn't this ancient writing that only dealt with issues thousands of years ago. As we studied the New Testament together, we discovered Christ's character. As we studied the Old Testament, we discovered many prophecies being fulfilled in the New Testament and current events today. We also discovered real human beings going through struggles and victories that we could relate to and glean wisdom from when we witnessed how God related to each person. Of course, our questions were never-ending, and there were a multitude of things we didn't understand. But, that is where faith interjected, and we trusted that God would reveal the meaning to us in time. His Word is eternal, and we all understood that we would be learning eternally. It was healthy to learn together because we could discuss, encourage, and challenge each other.

I found a life transformative routine in taking time to read God's Word daily, consider the context, and listen to how God was speaking to me through His Word. It is a vital necessity to my daily living.

ANN'S STORY

It all started with Ann and me doing a book club/kids playgroup. One day, while deciding what book to read next, I suggested, "How about a book in the Bible?" Who knew that "The Bible Babes" would grow so large that we'd need two groups?! We decided I would lead one and she the other. Here's Ann's story:

> God's Word began its work in me when I received a Bible from my 3rd grade confirmation in our Methodist church. We had to memorize Psalm 23. From the beginning, those words offered me comfort and peace as my mother fought and eventually lost a battle with cancer.
>
> When I accepted Jesus at 17, the first thing I did was pull out that unused Bible. I began to read it voraciously, attend Bible studies, and learn from mature believers. I memorized as much as I could, watched online pastors, and yearned to be transformed into the image of Christ. While my knowledge of God and His Word did make great advances during this time, I now realize that the work of the Holy Spirit does not conform to our efforts or timetables.
>
> Throughout my life, I have continued to cultivate my practice of ingesting God's Word. I have used online reading plans, devotionals, and read through the whole Bible several times. Sometimes I have been consistent and other times not. But God's Word has continued to inform my choices, challenge my attitudes, and shape my life.
>
> I cannot imagine life making sense without knowing God. His Word is the main source of

revelation of who God is. It is the breath of God. To me, it is the very essence of my life.

BECKY'S STORY

Becky was one of the first women to join us. She'd say, "I just wanted to get out of my house so I could get a break in the evening." I *loved* her transparency. I soon watched her entire family become transformed by God's Word and His love. Here's her story:

 I grew up in the Catholic church, and after getting married I found I was going less and less. I prayed at times growing up but really didn't understand or know how to have a personal relationship with God.

I was and am so blessed that I had a dear friend praying for me, and she brought me back to my faith. I started going to church with my family. Reluctantly, I started going to a Bible study run by this friend in her home. I can truly say the only reason I went is because she lived right down the block, and it was a way to be with women and a reason to leave my husband with our two very young children. Little did I know that this study would change my life. I learned how to have a personal and daily relationship with God which impacted me in so many ways —and also my family, especially our children. Since starting that study I have been in a weekly Bible study for almost 30 years.

It's been an amazing journey, and God has been there every step of the way. He promises to give me peace, strength, hope, encouragement, and the unconditional love that I feel every day. I have fallen many times, but He has been there to lift me up.

I am truly blessed that God answered my friend's prayer and set me on this beautiful journey of life with Him.

WE'VE GOT THE POWER

Many of us held a common misconception that wasn't addressed at church—it's that the Word of God has power! Hebrews 4:12 tells us that the Word is alive and active. Understanding that God's Word is truly powerful was essential to building up our faith. That it isn't just words on the page of a history book, but it is God breathed (2 Tim. 3:16), penned by men who were inspired by the Holy Spirit.

Also, God's spoken Word has creative power. For instance, God spoke the universe into existence.

Genesis 1:3: "And God said, 'Let there be light.'"

Genesis 1:6: "And God said, 'Let there be a firmament.'"

Genesis 1:9: "And God said, 'Let the waters separate from the land.'"

He spoke scripture to defeat the enemy. God could have used any form of weapon. Yet He chose scripture to be His power tool (Matt. 4:1-11).

HIS WORD HAS POWER

He cursed the fig tree (Mark 11:14). This reminds me of Proverbs 18:21 which says that life and death are in the power of the tongue. It also reminds me of God telling us that we have power and authority over His creation (Gen. 1:26). With power and authority, Jesus healed the centurion's son by a command (Matt. 8:5).

Recently, my 14-year-old daughter was scheduled for surgery for a torn tendon in her foot that occurred while she was playing soccer. I was praying that God would heal her foot immediately so she could compete in the soccer season as it had just begun. We were in the pre-op room and the surgeon said, "Let's just go take one more X-ray."

While they whisked her away, I pulled the curtain closed so the nurses wouldn't think I was crazy and grabbed my Bible. I turned to Matthew 8:5 and basically began "telling" or maybe praying, "Lord, this man didn't even know You as his Savior, but he knew the authority and power that You and Your Word had. So, I'm asking You like the centurion asked You to heal his servant, send forth Your healing power and heal my daughter's tendon in her foot so she doesn't have to have surgery today. In Jesus's name!"

I think I probably had some arms waving up and down and some pointing going on too. Ha! The doctor and my daughter came back to the pre-op room, and the doctor said, "I think we're just going to put her in a cast—she won't need surgery." Thank You, Lord! His Word is powerful. God tells us that we can speak to our mountains. Mark 11:23 says, "I tell you the truth, whoever says to this mountain, 'Be taken up and thrown into the sea,' and does not doubt in his heart but believes that what he says will come to pass, it will be done for him." This Scripture was immediately after Jesus cursed the fig tree. He tells His disciples in verse 22 to "have faith in God." Then He talks about the power of what we say can move mountains.

Understanding this truth increased our faith to memorize scripture and speak scripture over situations. Many times our situations looked opposite of what God's promises said, but we trusted in God's Word and "spoke it over our situations" as well as meditated on God's promises to keep us focused and at peace. It is a practice we had to choose to do every day. The more consistent we were in speaking God's truth, the more it built our faith. Faith comes from *hearing* the message, and the message is heard through the Word of Christ (Rom. 10:17).

As we learned to speak the Word of God over our situations, it increased our belief in God's promises and helped us stop focusing on our problems. In time, we saw God's promises manifest. His Word is powerful and goes out to accomplish what He promises when we agree with God and His Word. Satan knew we were serious and we were armed with God's Word to combat every lie and dart that he tried to throw at us. Sometimes we would see quick results, and sometimes situations would take years for God's promises to manifest. Some issues we are still professing God's Word over and believe that in due time we will see the promises come to fruition.

THE WORD HAS POWER—IT WORKS!

It works! It reminds me of a product for weight loss called "IT WORKS." I'm a sucker for "As seen on TV" products. I am always so curious if "it works." A friend of mine was selling a product with natural oils and herbs that would detox your body and "BOOM!" you would instantly see weight loss results. The instructions said to rub this gel in the area where you needed to lose a few inches and then wrap the area with plastic wrap for 20 to 30 minutes, and *ta-dah*, your shape would be minimized. Keep in mind that the product continued to work for at least a few hours after applying it because the product permeated your skin.

I decided one evening before going out to an event that I would try "IT WORKS"! I went upstairs and locked myself in the bathroom, rubbed the gel from my stomach to my knees, front and backside. Then I took the box of plastic wrap and wrapped it around my stomach and legs several times. I now had to figure out how I was going to shuffle to my bed and lie down so the product could soak in and do its job. I looked like a polish sausage scurrying from the bathroom to somehow shimmy my legs onto the bed while plastic wrapped together. I cannot even imagine if my husband had come into the bedroom to see what I was doing.

Thirty minutes was up and I rolled off the bed and shuffled back into the bathroom to unwrap my body. I showered the gel off and *voila*! I was convinced that the product was at work and I was going to see my shape minimized. I proceeded to get dressed for a festive evening out with six couples—a nice dinner out and then off to The Nutcracker ballet to follow. While eating dinner, I started to get warm and wondered, *Is this what a hot flash feels like?* The heat began to grow, and then I began to itch and sweat.

When we were seated at The Nutcracker, beads of sweat were rolling down my body. I felt like I was on fire from my stomach to my knees. I was thinking, *How in the world am I going to make it through this ballet? What is going on with my body?* Then it dawned on me. "IT WORKS" was work-ing! Then I realized I had to sit through the longest and weirdest ballet known to mankind while itching, sweating, and on fire because I had to test "IT WORKS!" What in the world was I going to tell my husband? "Um, honey... we need to leave because I just rubbed this product called "IT WORKS" all over my body before we came here, and I'm having an allergic reaction to the herbs and gel. I want to crawl out of my skin!" I was imagining one of the ballerinas seeing smoke coming out of my ears and breaking out singing Alicia Keys' song, *That girl is on Fi-yahhh!*

Guess what? God's Word WORKS!

WHAT I'M GLAD I LEARNED

If I were to take a survey with the women who studied God's Word in these groups, I think we would concur that we would have never grown in our faith and relationship with Jesus if we hadn't had God's Word planted in our hearts and considered it to be a vital necessity in our daily living. We discovered God's Truth indeed sets you free (John 8:32). The more our relationship grew with Jesus, and the more His Word was planted in our hearts, the more we became set free from ourselves, strongholds, wrong thinking patterns, health issues, relationships, and destructive habits that held us in bondage.

We all learned that God's Word is reliable, powerful, and a vital necessity for living an abundant life as a Christian, and the Word solidified our relationship with Jesus as we came to understand it is God Himself speaking to us.

SELAH

Do you have situations in your life that could use some powerful transformation?

Find a promise that pertains to your situation and begin to speak over it with God's Word. There is power in consistency. As we speak God's Word, it increases our faith, and it releases God's powerful Word into the spiritual realm and doesn't come back void (Isa. 55:11). It works!

Lastly, is God's Word essential to your faith? Is it more precious than gold to you?

Joshua 1:8 says, "Keep this Book of the Law always on your lips; meditate on it day and night, so that you may be careful to do everything written in it. Then you will be prosperous and successful."

Chapter 7
I DIDN'T LEARN THAT HEALING IS FOR TODAY

DOES HE HEAL TODAY?

> "Jesus called his twelve disciples to him and gave them authority to drive out impure spirits and to heal every disease and sickness... Heal the sick, raise the dead, cleanse those who have leprosy, drive out demons. Freely you have received; freely give" (Matt. 10:1-8).

> "Jesus went through all the towns and villages, teaching in their synagogues, proclaiming the good news of the kingdom and healing every disease and sickness" (Matt. 9:35).

MY STORY

I recall that first gathering in our home at age 30, reading through the Gospel of Mark. I was so excited to see that Jesus went about healing. It gave me hope that if in biblical days He healed, then He certainly would do it today. But why hadn't I heard about healing miracles in church? It seemed so wrong in my spirit that a loving Father would want His child to be sick to "teach him something." I was open-minded and such a freshman when I approached the scriptures. I was struck at how many times He said, "Your faith made you well." Faith? Faith in the truth that God wanted me well? Sickness is not from God? Is it always God's will for man to be healthy? Sickness and disease are from the enemy?

What? These were foreign truths to me. Many mainstream Christians weren't comfortable buying into these truths 100%. Cessationists believe that all miracles ceased for today and were just active in biblical times. That seemed preposterous to me and out of character for the Jesus I was reading about in the scriptures. A cessationist probably never witnessed a miracle because you must first believe a miracle can even happen. Many of the people I encountered in my church growing up were comfortable saying, "Well, if it is God's will, then you will be healed."

I have heard many pastors that teach on healing say, "If it is God's will for you to be sick, then why do you go to a doctor to get well? Stay in God's will and be sick so you can learn something." As a dear friend of mine would say—B.S! Wrong *Belief System*.

I needed to renew my mind to the truth in God's Word about healing. God wanted me well and I could receive healing from Him. That is what I needed faith in.

> "But, he was pierced for our transgressions, he was crushed for our iniquities; the punishment that brought us peace was on him, and by his wounds we are healed" (Isa. 53:5).

I began to study the scriptures fervently and not only renewed my mind to His healing promises about spiritual and emotional healing but I started to receive revelation knowledge in my heart about Jesus physically healing us at the Cross. He bore our sins and iniquities and made us righteous through the shedding of His blood. Then He gave us a divine exchange of new life. He also beat the curse of sickness and disease. Jesus took on sickness and disease in His body and beat it at the Cross. He beat what the enemy loves to bestow upon God's children. By faith, we can receive healing from Him and see healing manifest in our bodies. "By His stripes we are healed" (Isa. 53:5). Notice it says, "We *are...*" It's prophesying that we were healed at the Cross, and now we need to renew our minds to the truth and receive what He did on the Cross for us.

I recall a woman in that first Bible study walking out because I was declaring this simple truth. She obviously was offended by what I was teaching. God wants you well, and healing is always there for the believer. She was offended by that "absurd" truth. Maybe she had been wounded by an illness herself or a family member had been dealing with a chronic illness? Maybe it was just "too simplistic" and not intellectual enough to believe in a truth like that? I, however, was elated to come across this truth because I was suffering from insomnia and postpartum depression, and it gave me hope.

I also recall being so excited about this truth that I presented it to my pastor at that time. I sat down in his office and showed him the Scripture in Mark 5:34 where Jesus healed the woman with the issue of blood. He was highly intellectual and graciously listened to me. He then went on to encourage me that "it just isn't that simple." I was so discouraged when I left his office. I was struggling with postpartum depression trudging through each day with insomnia and despair. I so desired for the well-educated Ph.D. scholarly pastor to confirm that "by His stripes I was healed" was the truth and to teach me how to receive healing.

THE STUDY AND SEARCH CONTINUED

After that discouraging meeting with the pastor, I went on a search for 20 years, trying to grasp healing. Many times I would fall into self-effort and try real hard to "get healed" by rebuking the devil, professing I was healed, and then getting discouraged when I saw no difference in my body. I realized I didn't have a revelation of healing like I had with salvation. I could say that I truly believed I was saved, but I didn't have that same depth of belief that God healed me at the Cross. I could receive it and agree with God's promise that what He did at the Cross concerning my health was available to me. I studied healing more and more. I desired to see the healings I read about in the scriptures come to life in the present day. God was very gracious as He taught me. He healed me incrementally throughout bouts of post-partum depression with each of our five kids. The last bout was the most intense and I was so thankful I had the truth in my heart about God's will for me to be whole and healthy and that He indeed died and took on the effects of sin and sickness in His body so I could be whole. I was also thankful I had an incredible support system through doctors, prayer warriors, friends, and family—especially my husband.

CAROLINE'S HEALING

Our daughter was almost one when she was scheduled to get tubes in her ears for chronic ear infections. I was getting frustrated because I was learning about healing and praying for God to heal Caroline's ears, but to no result. One night, I had it in my heart to just go to her crib and lay my hand on her ears and simply profess what God had done on the Cross for Caroline and ask God to manifest healing in her ears. All the while, I was asking the group to pray and believe with me. I could tell many were like, "Okay?" It's just a simple procedure. It's not like it's a disease; kids get it done all the time. But, I was like, *Show me the money, Lord! I want to see Your truth come to fruition.* About 3 a.m. the morning before her surgery I heard her crying and went into her room. I could tell she had a fever and was uncomfortable. I was bummed and disappointed, thinking, *Well I tried. Maybe next time I can witness God's healing.* I went back to sleep.

I got a clear revelation in my spirit. She has a fever, so she won't be able to have surgery that morning. I prayed, "God, I believe You are going to heal her." I had to run her to the pediatrician that morning, and on the way, I ran into one of the women in the group. I was so excited to tell her that I believed God was going to heal Caroline's ears. I sensed she thought I was a little cuckoo. Satan was still trying to get me to doubt on the way to the doctor's office. However, I dismissed the skeptical look from my friend and proceeded to the doctor's appointment.

We got into the appointment and the doctor looked in Caroline's ears with the otoscope and said, "Her ears are crystal clear, she doesn't need surgery."

I wanted to jump up, high-five the doctor, and tell him that I had been praying for healing, etc... but, I refrained and said, "Thank God!"

CARTER'S HEALING

I also recall a time when one of our boys was playing basketball in elementary school. He went to block a lay-up and slammed down onto the gym floor with his forearm under his body. My husband took him to the ER for an X-ray, and it revealed that he had a fracture. We made an appointment to see a hand specialist the following day. While in the office, I had another stirring in my heart. My conversation (or maybe somewhat complaint) in my head was, "Lord, You healed instantly all the time in the scriptures. Your Word says, 'By Your stripes we are healed.' I believe Your Word to be true; would You please show me that it is true?" The doctor had a copy of the X-ray and saw the picture of the fracture. He examined my son's forearm and looked puzzled because my son wasn't feeling pain or discomfort in the area where the fracture had occurred. The doctor then said, "Let's take another X-ray." He looked at the X-ray, and there wasn't a fracture. Again, I wanted to scream, "Hallelujah!" But, I think I may have said, "Praise God!" It was a wonderful testimony to share with my son and family about watching God's healing power manifest.

MICHELE'S ASK

My kids and husband all knew I was very passionate about the subject of healing in the scriptures. One evening my friend Michele called to ask me to pray for our mutual neighbor. Michele was in our neighborhood Bible study. It wasn't uncommon for the women in the group to request prayer for others. But I never thought this prayer request would also be a call to action.

The neighbors were a married couple in their early 40s with three kids similar in age to ours. The couple was on a date playing soccer. He was very fit and an avid runner. He suddenly had a brain aneurysm and was rushed to the ICU and put on life support. My kids overheard my phone conversation with Michele and a couple of them said, "Mom, you know about healing—why don't you call Mrs. Becker and ask if you can pray over Mr. Becker?" I thought, *No, I'm good; I can just pray for him right here in the comfort of my home.* I was thinking of every way to get out of it. First of all, how awkward? We knew the Beckers socially, and they were great neighbors, but this situation was very personal and sensitive. A situation for which I wanted to highly respect their privacy.

Also, they were Jewish, and I wasn't sure they would welcome me coming over and laying hands on Michael. But I prayed and got that deep nudging to let them know I was willing to come to pray over Michael if his wife, Laura, was open to it. I think I even closed my eyes as I told Michele to mention it to Laura because I was embarrassed and self-conscious as to what Laura might think of me. *So selfless of me to be thinking about myself and my reputation when a dear neighbor's husband is in a life-threatening state* (eye roll). Shortly after, I got a phone call from Michele reporting that it wasn't looking good at all and that Michael's brain activity was declining. The family had flown in, their rabbi was with them at the hospital, and they were debating what steps to take next.

Michele also said, "Laura would like you to come and pray over Michael."

Oh, wow! We had a couple of friends that had been in ministry for quite some time who believed and had witnessed many miraculous healings *and even witnessed a couple people being raised from the dead!* (If I could put an emoji in this sentence, it would be the face with the two bulging eyes.) Well, again I prayed, and I felt led to ask those friends to come with me.

Now, imagine the somber waiting room outside the ICU where Michael and Laura's closest Jewish relatives and friends were gathering. Here walked these three strange Gentiles coming to pray over Michael. One of the women pulled me aside, and with her thick New York accent asked, "What's your success rate?" Oh my goodness, what pressure! I had only witnessed some ears being healed and a fracture disappearing, and was just offering to come to pray because my kids shamed me into it; now all of these grief-stricken family and friends think we are going to usher in some miracle!

Laura escorted us to Michael's room. I was taken aback seeing him with tubes running everywhere, his head and face swollen and bandaged up. The doctors mentioned that if his numbers got to a certain point, he could have a chance of regaining normal brain function. By conventional wisdom, this could only happen by a miracle. So I nervously said to my prayer warrior friends, "You go first." I was stunned at the gravity of the situation that God had placed us in. It wasn't comfortable at all and I was hoping I wouldn't freeze. Because my friends were seasoned prayer warriors, I wanted them to lead the prayer while I just stood back in agreement. We prayed fervently for my friend and read scripture over Michael. The numbers on the monitor began to gradually move in a positive direction. The power of prayer was having an impact on Michael's physical body. The numbers on the monitor were an indication of Michael's brain function working.

Then we learned that the family was nervous that we were in the room with Michael—what if he passed while we were at his bedside and they were not? We came out of the ICU room, but my friend really felt in his spirit that if we could pray a couple more times, we would see further progress. Laura courageously coerced her in-laws and the rabbi to allow us to go back into Michael's room, and my friend started speaking to Michael. He said, "Michael, you are one of the chosen, you have the Old Covenant, and Christ died for you; choose Christ and fulfill the New Covenant in your life." As we looked at Michael's face, we noticed a tear trickling down his cheek. Simultaneously, Laura walked into the room and saw the tear. She gently wiped it away and kissed his cheek. She told us that the family wanted to come in again.

We were excited, but my friend wanted to go back into the room to pray some more because he sensed that God was healing Michael. My friend had the gift of seeing in the spiritual realm (another thing I *never* learned at church). In the spiritual realm, he saw God's hand reaching down and saw Jesus's body lying on Michael. We weren't allowed to go back into his room, and shortly after they took Michael off of life support. However, that image of Jesus lying on Michael spoke to us deeply that he was saved that afternoon as we prayed. His earthly body wasn't healed, but the Lord healed him eternally and gave him new life in Christ.

That was such a teaching moment for me. I learned to never underestimate the power of God's Word and how one can receive salvation even while in a subconscious or near-death state. That day Michael's spirit was renewed eternally. This was definitely something I didn't learn at church! Thankfully, in that moment of crisis, Michele had been gracious

and bold enough to offer our ministry of prayer to the family
—I believe God used it to change Michael's eternal destiny.

ANOTHER NEIGHBOR?

Several years later, I was in another neighborhood Bible
study with a strong group of faith-filled women. We all
asked the Lord to place people on our hearts that may need
prayer for healing. Someone in the group asked me if I knew
her friend in my neighborhood who was currently in the
ICU struggling with a rare type of cancer. She was in her
late forties, previously a very active woman, and had two
college-aged children and a wonderful husband. I replied,
"You know what? 'Coincidently' I ran into a neighbor
yesterday while walking our dogs, and she told me to pray
for our neighbor Elaine who was in the ICU struggling with
a rare type of cancer."

I left our Bible study and couldn't get Elaine off of my heart.
The following week, while showering and praying, I felt an
urgency to go to the ICU and pray for Elaine. I got out of
the shower and saw a text from one of the women in our
gathering that knew Elaine. She was texting me that she had
it in her heart to go to the hospital and pray for Elaine too.
Well, that was confirmation!

It was Wednesday morning and we were meeting in an
hour. We arrived at our gathering for Bible study and I
proposed we drive downtown to the hospital and go pray for
Elaine. We contacted Elaine's husband and he got clearance
from the ICU nursing staff. Several of us went into Elaine's
room. We sang worship songs, prayed over her, and took
communion while Elaine lay intubated in the ICU. Her
husband had told us that the best-case scenario was that she
would be able to leave the ICU in three weeks if all went

well. Two days later we heard a report from our neighbor that she was home. God put the desire in our hearts to go out and lay hands on the sick (James 5:14). He allowed us to see His healing power manifest in Elaine.

HEALING IN HAITI

God anointed Jesus of Nazareth with the Holy Spirit and with power. "Then Jesus went around doing good and healing all who were oppressed by the devil, for God was with him" (Acts 10:38).

A few years ago, I was blessed to go on a mission trip to Haiti. The small group I went with had traveled to Haiti on several occasions ministering to people in a remote area for many years. I was anxious to witness God's supernatural power in Haiti because the group of people I traveled with had seen God do many miracles there. This particular group of people also believed what Jesus spoke of in Mark 16. Seeing the Haitians' openness to God's healing power and the supernatural was beautiful. I believe they don't have the opportunity to always go to a doctor right away, so their first go-to for healing is God. Witchcraft is prevalent there and they are aware of the power of the supernatural, whether it be in the demonic or Christian realm. Therefore, I believe it may be easier for them to receive healing and miracles from God. They don't have to renew their minds regarding God's desire and ability to heal and do signs and wonders and undo wrong thinking regarding God's super-natural power.

Towards the end of the week, we had an opportunity to go minister to a young man in his twenties. The family said he was in a trance state, hadn't walked in several months, and wasn't of sound mind. The dear pastor I traveled with knew how I so desired to see God's healing power at work, so he asked me to come along to pray over this young man.

We arrived at the family's thatched roof home. Chickens, goats, and cats were running freely in the small patch of grass that was their front yard. I thought, *Well, Jesus rebuked the demons into the pigs. Are we going to rebuke the demon of this young man into the chickens?* Johnny the pastor, his wife, an interpreter, and I approached the young man sitting in a chair with his legs stretched out frozen in front of him. He was tormented. Johnny began praying and professing the gospel to this young man. The young man was quite restless, and each time Johnny said the name "Jesus" he became even more agitated. My heart was pounding a bit because I had never witnessed a demon-oppressed person. The family had explained that the young man used to read the Bible but had been going to visit the local witch doctor weekly, and was now in this incoherent and paralyzed state.

We all prayed over him; Johnny commanded the demon to leave him with gentle authority. There was a bit of struggle with the young man as he waved his arms and struggled to let go, but Johnny kept professing the name of Jesus over him. Then shortly thereafter, the young man was at peace. Johnny shared the gospel message with him and the young man accepted Christ. The interpreter actually poured a bottle of water over his head to baptize him. You do what ya gotta do!

As we were getting ready to leave, I had a strong nudge that we needed to pray for physical healing over him and command what was paralyzing him to be gone and watch this young man walk. I felt intimidated and wondered, *What if it doesn't work and I'm chiming in with this stupid idea?* But, we all agreed, and with great authority, the Haitian interpreter commanded the young man to be healed and to get out of the chair and walk. Praise God, that young man got out of the chair and began walking around the yard with the chickens and goats! His family was smiling ear to ear. I was elated and thought, *Okay, what do we do now, just say, "See ya later and good luck"?*

But, as you look at Jesus and the disciples, they went about doing good and healing all who were oppressed by illness and demons, and they moved on from village to village. Again, I wasn't in church learning this. I was with *THE* Church—the Body of Christ—learning what Jesus taught us to do and using the authority He gave us. Freely you receive. Freely you give.

WHAT I'M GLAD I LEARNED

God's desire is for us to be well—physically, spiritually, and emotionally.

Satan's desire is for us to be sick—physically, spiritually, and emotionally.

Some healings come instantly, and some take time to manifest.

Agreeing and professing God's promises regarding healing for my life and others' lives has power and can manifest healing.

God doesn't put sickness on us to teach us something!

When sickness tries to come against me, I combat it with the truth. God died for us to be whole. As I wait upon Him and receive from Him, I know in my head and heart that He is working and willing to give me health.

SELAH

Have you ever experienced God's healing? Physically? Spiritually? Emotionally?

Do you believe God wants you well?

Do you believe sickness is not put on us by God to "teach" us something?

Do you believe sickness, disease, and tormenting spirits are from the enemy?

Do you believe the resurrection power of Jesus Christ lives in you, and you too can be healed and live in divine health by His power?

Chapter 8
ON HIS MARK. GET SET. GO!

ON WHOSE MARK?

When Jesus died on the Cross He said, "It is finished." He conquered death and sin on the Cross. He conquered evil. Satan himself. He took on our guilt, shame, condemnation, judgment, sickness, and sin. He finished it! He rose and gave us victory. Victory to live in freedom every day and to experience "His will here on earth as it is in Heaven." For His will to be done here on earth as it is in Heaven, He needs vessels—us, His children, walking in the authority and freedom He gave us. Our starting place—our MARK—is victorious. Our starting place is no longer what was handed down to us, the abuses we suffered, or the consequences of poor choices we've made. We now *start* in the place of freedom and forgiveness. Buried with Him in His death, we are raised with Him in His eternal life. We are seated with Him in heavenly places (Eph. 2:6). Our position (or starting place) as a Christian is in the Victor! Jesus, though not guilty, took "our mark" of sin on Himself 2000 years ago and was persecuted, spat on, mocked, tortured, and bludgeoned to death.

He took 39 marks on His back for our wholeness. And now, "on His mark," we are positioned to live a life of freedom.

Do we live in a mindset of the true gospel where Jesus took our sin and we are truly forgiven and redeemed? Do we have the mindset that we have authority over the enemy daily?

WHAT IS YOUR MIND SET ON?

Do we have our minds SET on the truth daily? Is the true meaning of the gospel and what Christ did for us set in our inner deepest being? Or do we simply have the "mark" of salvation (believing we will spend eternity with Christ) without applying the marks He took for us on the Cross into our daily lives?

In this world, our thinking is challenged minute by minute. Because of this, our minds must be set on truth to live in victory. Victorious mindsets of truths from God's Word are: I am saved, I am redeemed from the curse, I am healed, I am delivered—delivered from addictions, a critical spirit, procrastination, drugs, shopping, food, porn, (you fill in the blank); because if we are honest, we all have things in our lives that we have needed to be delivered from.

I am the righteousness of God in Jesus Christ. I am patient. I am kind. I am courageous. I am prosperous. I can do all things through Christ. When we get our minds set, it allows us to live the life of freedom for which Christ died for us. "As a man thinks so he is" (Prov. 23:7). It is living according to the Spirit and not by our feelings or circumstances. If Christ had lived merely by His feelings, all of us would be going to hell! He wouldn't have fulfilled God's will if He'd decided to listen to the enemy when He was in the Garden of Gethsemane sweating tears of blood. Jesus's mind had to be set on truth. When we go through persecution and trials we must get our minds set on what Christ already provided for us at the Cross.

Speak it and stand on it.

Maybe you are wondering if you are "set." Do I really believe that Christ took my sin, shame, and sickness on the Cross and died for me to have a life full of joy even amid trials? Do I really believe the gospel message? Or do I believe I have to earn my salvation and do something for God to accept me? Friends, that isn't freedom. That isn't the true gospel. There is nothing we can "do" for God to accept us but believe and receive His grace and gift of salvation.

GO

> "Therefore GO and make disciples of all nations, baptizing them in the name of the Father and of the Son and of the Holy Spirit" (Matt. 28:19).

Jesus told the twelve apostles to go out and share what He had done for all people.

MY STORY

A couple of years ago, my husband and I attended the funeral of one of the women who attended the first Bible study I had in our home in Chicago. When the service concluded, some women that I recognized but couldn't place came up to me. They introduced themselves and reminded me that they were in the Bible studies that continued from the first gathering. It clicked. Their stories and faces were back in our family room over twenty years ago.

Some of us reconnected and had a girl's weekend in Chicago. It was a wild one! We ordered Chinese food, shared what God had been doing in our lives, and two of the women even got water baptized in the bathtub of our friend's condo in downtown Chicago.

Like the twelve disciples, we "went out" alright! They shared how they had "gone out" with families and friends and discipled them to grow in Christ.

All from a desire to know God's truth and grow in His love some twenty-plus years ago.

KATIE'S STORY

Katie's back...

> I was at the end of myself—exactly where I needed to be for God to reach me. The life I imagined as a wife and new mother was not turning out as I had planned, and I could not figure out a solution on my own. After sharing parts of my struggle with a close friend, she invited me to join her at a neighborhood Bible study. My first thought was, *I will never go, I am not one of those churchy women, and we will have nothing in common.* After her numerous invitations, I agreed to join her—just once. I had never owned a Bible, wasn't familiar with Christian teaching, and the "Christianese" (terms like "God's leading" and "blessed life" that some of the women used

were so odd to me), yet I wanted to go again the next week.

The women in the group were pretty, well-dressed, successful, and, what I deemed in my shallow assessment, to be women who could be my friends. And so my adventure began. I continued to go every week, and for months I didn't understand what I was reading in the Bible, or even how to find a chapter or a verse in that thick book. But I felt an unbelievable, unexplainable peace during that dark time. Week after week the other women shared their hearts, their struggles, prayer requests, the answers to their prayers, and how God was working in their lives... I wanted what they had.

About six months in, while working on my Bible study at home and in tears, still unable to understand the deeper meaning and connections the other ladies could find in the Bible verses, and feeling like my home life was collapsing in around me, I prayed my first authentic prayer: "If in fact You, God, are real, help me. I am not the master of my life as I thought; I cannot live like this anymore, and I need You." And He did reveal Himself—in circumstances, Bible verses that reached deep in my heart, friendships—in the start of some and the ending of others. What I enjoyed and desired began to change, His gentle promptings about how I was living my life then led to making those changes. I had hope and felt the unexplainable peace and the incredible love that He had for me. And now after 25 years, our relationship continues to deepen. My situation hasn't magically turned around, but in the midst of life's challenges, He has faithfully encouraged me while giving me hope and purpose. He has softened my heart. Over the years I have seen His hand in countless circumstances which is often all I need—to know He is always with me. God is the only thing I know for certain, and I am overwhelmed with gratitude for Him saving me from myself.

MICHELE'S STORY

Michele was in a neighborhood women's group that I led in Michigan. Being raised Catholic, she would say that attending a Bible study and a megachurch were both foreign to her. I remember walking up the stairs of that church with her one Saturday and hearing, "I don't think my husband would ever step foot in this place." In my heart I thought, *You never know what God can do.* Fast forward a few years later, her husband and three kids all attended that megachurch, found Christ, and are strong in their faith. She tells the story:

 I would like to offer insight into what kind of person I was BIKC (Before I Knew Christ). I did not subscribe to the belief system of having a "God-centered life." Frankly, I doubted the existence of any god. This was my well-kept secret, paramount as a solid member of my traditional Catholic family. Reaching the age of 28 and a decade with my husband felt like the right time for me to relent and forego my body's "ideal figure." However, this was simultaneously the point I had perfected "exercise bulimia" well enough to bring about its natural consequence of infertility. As an overachiever, I controlled every aspect of my life and the lives of those who would tolerate it. My husband, John, and I invested most of our time in self-serving, over-indulgent activities which had finally reached the (now obvious) outcomes of boredom and unfulfillment. The culturally-expected next step was to start our family. I was about 80% on board. Sure, why not?

What began as a surrendering of my ideal body weight quickly transformed into a full-blown obsession—tracking every mile run and bite consumed in hopes of pregnancy. Following 12 failed months, we accepted the reality of needing outside help. John and I contacted a well-known medical professional who specializes in infertility. This began our 3-year quest to have a baby.

Looking back, it is comical to me the extent to which narcissistic people like myself will go to achieve a self-serving goal. Pregnancy occupied my every thought. Concluding after another "wasted" year that I had exhausted all options, I pivoted, turning toward a god I was unsure existed. This birthed the beginning of "The Negotiation." I began audibly bargaining, "If you give me a baby, then I will..." Those tactics proved unsuccessful, so I stepped it up. What began as polite directives to God morphed into something desperate and ugly. One particularly defining memory involved my yelling at the Creator of the Universe, "I am a good person! I deserve this! Why won't You give this to me!?" Eventually, I settled down and posed questions rather than demands: "I am a good person, right God? I deserve this, don't I?"

And so the pruning began. He patiently waited, trimming and molding, until I was truly ready to see Him, to hear Him regardless of what He could offer. My focus finally shifted from me to Him, from us to God. God painstakingly changed a marriage we loved into one designed as His. Three years of doctor visits, failed treatments, and mounting debt moved us to just the right place: one where we could humbly receive Him.

And so it happened.

Our fertility doctor said my initial blood results definitely did not indicate multiples, yet the news of our twin pregnancy was of no surprise to me. I had asked for twins and had no reason to believe He would deny me twins. The first ultrasound was one of my "never forget" moments. John's reaction was priceless. From a sitting position, he stood, then sat, then stood, then sat! Sounding half-crazed, he remarked, "I don't know if I should get my butt back to work or the golf course!" John and I celebrated the news of my pregnancy with immeasurable gratitude, and more so, a thankfulness for the experiences of getting there.

My water broke 8 1/2 weeks early on Thanksgiving. The irony was not lost on me. Emily and Nicholas weighed in at a combined weight of 6.5 pounds. It was without a doubt the best day of my life, but not for the reasons you would think. That day marked my complete transformation. I could literally feel Him—in an undeniable moment so palatable and intimate I could not discern if it was coming *from* me or *to* me.

Fast forward four years.

The memory of that unforgettable day was still alive yet faded just enough to resume my selfish momentum. Life was now about Him and Me and Me and Him. I wanted another baby. I needed another baby. Why not, I deserved it, right? I loved God and recognized His voice, but Controllers like me control, not trust. I couldn't risk "unanswered" prayer. I had to take over, you know, *help out* with suggestions as to how He could proceed.

John, on the other hand, had had enough. We had already invested another year towards failed attempts and spent money we did not have. John was selling contentment, but I was not buying. He agreed to one last round, and this was my final chance. Back then, hormone therapy was typically one vial a day leading up to two, then three. I decided this conservative approach was far too risky. When our fertility specialist scripted one vial, I shot two. When scripting two, I shot three. I wasn't interested in knowing the associated health risks of such reckless behavior.

Not surprisingly, our doctor was taken aback by the results of this final round. Certainly seven mature follicles, as with my twin pregnancy, were to be expected. However, this final ultrasound showed 27 *mature follicles*. Self-medicating had paid off... assuming I didn't die. Our doctor's professional recommendation was to "aspirate" all but five. All I heard was a suggestion to throw away 22 babies. John and I faced a monumental decision. We were excited about the probability of getting pregnant but truthfully unprepared to go from a family of four to ten. We prayed aloud together for the first time in our marriage. The answer was clear.

To say our decision was received unfavorably would be putting it mildly. The doc's enormous ego would not allow us to place his medical reputation at risk with multiple births. He said he "was not going to be one of those irresponsible physicians seen on television." We weren't budging. Our decision was final. Prior to the final procedure of fertilization, John and I were handed a document relieving his practice of any malpractice should our pregnancy result in multiples. No problem, we didn't need him. We had HIM. Rather than performing the final procedure himself, our doc assigned it to a nurse. Again, no problem.

Would it be a spoiler to jump to the end? Aidan was born 2.5 weeks premature on the twins' birthday, Thanksgiving weekend. We had received permission from our OB/GYN to schedule Aidan's C-section on that day. Arriving at the hospital for the procedure, the nurse on duty asked how long I had been experiencing contractions. Contractions!? Not to be out-controlled, hours before the surgical procedure, God had apparently initiated my labor, and I had mistaken the "discomfort" for nervousness. Evidently, I needed to be metaphorically hit over the head to recognize His hand. Nice play. God has a sense of humor. Who knew? So should we have been guests on Oprah? Sounds cool. Would the real message be lost on some? Probably. But what is really cool is when I get to share the backstory about the lost sheep pursued by a powerful God. I thought I was unworthy of His time. But now I finally understood grace. I was, and never would be, good enough. Turns out none of us are.

WHAT I'M GLAD I LEARNED

I'm so grateful that I learned salvation (His **MARK**) was more than a ticket to Heaven after this life here on earth. I'm thankful, I *finally* have a revelation that salvation is a gift of grace. I don't have to "earn" my salvation through my behavior. I was accepted, forgiven, and made righteous in Christ the minute I accepted Him into my life. I actually received a new identity when I accepted Christ as my Lord.

My position in Christ (aka On His Mark) didn't change when I messed up. I am glad I learned that God is patient and kind. That He gave me the Holy Spirit as my Helper who walks with me daily when I am challenged to keep my mind **SET** on everything that is true and lovely. I'm so glad that I have the opportunity to **GO** out and share the good news and see lives transformed by God's immeasurable love, word, grace, and power. There is no greater gift!

SELAH

Do you have His "mark" of salvation?

What "marks" you as a believer?

What "marks" can you identify that Christ took for you on the Cross?

What "marks" are like thorns in your side from which you're not sure you will ever be delivered?

What is your mind "set" on daily?

Have you ever "gone" out and shared what Christ has done for you?

Where would you like to "go" and share God's message of salvation?

If you've never prayed to receive Jesus into your life *or* would like a guide for leading someone else to pray, here is a suggested prayer of salvation:

Heavenly Father, I believe that Jesus Christ, the only begotten Son of God came to earth to be the Savior of the world and that by His death on the Cross, He paid the price for the sin of the world, so that whosoever believes in Him would not perish, but have everlasting life (John 3:16).

Thank You for Jesus, and thank You for my free gift of salvation. Thank You that by believing in His name, I am forgiven of all my sins and brought into sweet fellowship with You, Heavenly Father.

Thank You, Lord, for sending Your Son to die on the Cross in my place. Thank You that His innocent life took all the marks of my sin and His blood sacrifice was sufficient to pay the full price for my sin, and the sin of the world.

Lord, I turn from all my prideful sins and from everything that is dishonoring to You, and pray that I would grow in grace and in a knowledge of Jesus, until I come to a spiritual maturity, as day by day the Holy Spirit seeks to transform me into the likeness of Jesus. Thank You, Father God, for Your wonderful gift of salvation, and thank You that by believing, I am now Your child. In Jesus's name I pray,

Amen.

Chapter 9
CONCLUSION

I was just seeking to do something different in our book club/playgroup 25-plus years ago when this all started. God took seeking-Becky and set me on a path. Had I known all the wild rides ahead of me I might have never said yes, but along with all the challenges, He brought so many amazing relationships—I was able to see lives changed, renewed, set free from bondages, and numerous families restored to Christ. I'm so incredibly thankful.

Many of us gleaned a lot of truths of God from our church experiences, but some of the most vital life-changing revelations came outside of the normal "church" environment— God teaching us lessons one on one in our gatherings— through His blessings or through the crucible of difficult situations, even through spiritual warfare. Not surprisingly, we see this template in the Gospels. Jesus teaching, living, communing with 12 hungry disciples, hungry for truth. In the book of Acts, many met in homes breaking bread, reading scripture, and praying together. Maybe, just maybe, that's why it was fruitful. God's template always works.

Don't underestimate what God will do if you'll simply say yes.

So is He calling you to join together with some friends, share life, and seek Him?

Let me encourage you to do it! Start *today* learning and sharing what you didn't learn in church.

Grab a journal and process the following transformative truths outside the pew.

You'll find a richness of kingdom living that I believe He intended you to experience.

1. Now that you know what we "didn't learn in church," do you feel similarly?
2. Did you notice some of those same topics missing from your time in church?
3. Which stories could you relate to?
4. What transformative truths of God's Word have you learned outside the pew?
5. Do you have a desire to nurture and develop a deeper understanding of them?
6. Do you have a desire to gather and grow with others around those truths?

About the Author

From haute couture to house church, Rebecca Hitchcock's story is one of transformation and faith.

Rebecca spent nearly a decade directing fashion shows for Marshall Field's, overseeing all aspects of fashion show production, scouting models, coordinating fashion looks, and serving as a national media spokesperson. Rebecca's career in this intense fashion industry was nothing short of The-Devil-Wears-Prada-esque.

Throughout her career, Rebecca collaborated with many well-known designers, personalities, celebs, and supermodels. Although her career was challenging and exciting she always had an inkling that there was more in store for her.

She now lives in Indiana with her husband, Cam, with whom she has five children: Connor and his wonderful wife Christa, Caroline and her wonderful husband Michael, Carter, Cameron, and Claudia. Rebecca loves reading, walking, traveling, cooking and eating out! As a student of the Word for 28 years, she is passionate about sharing God's truth with other women and seeing their lives transformed by His powerful Word.

Made in the USA
Columbia, SC
02 November 2022